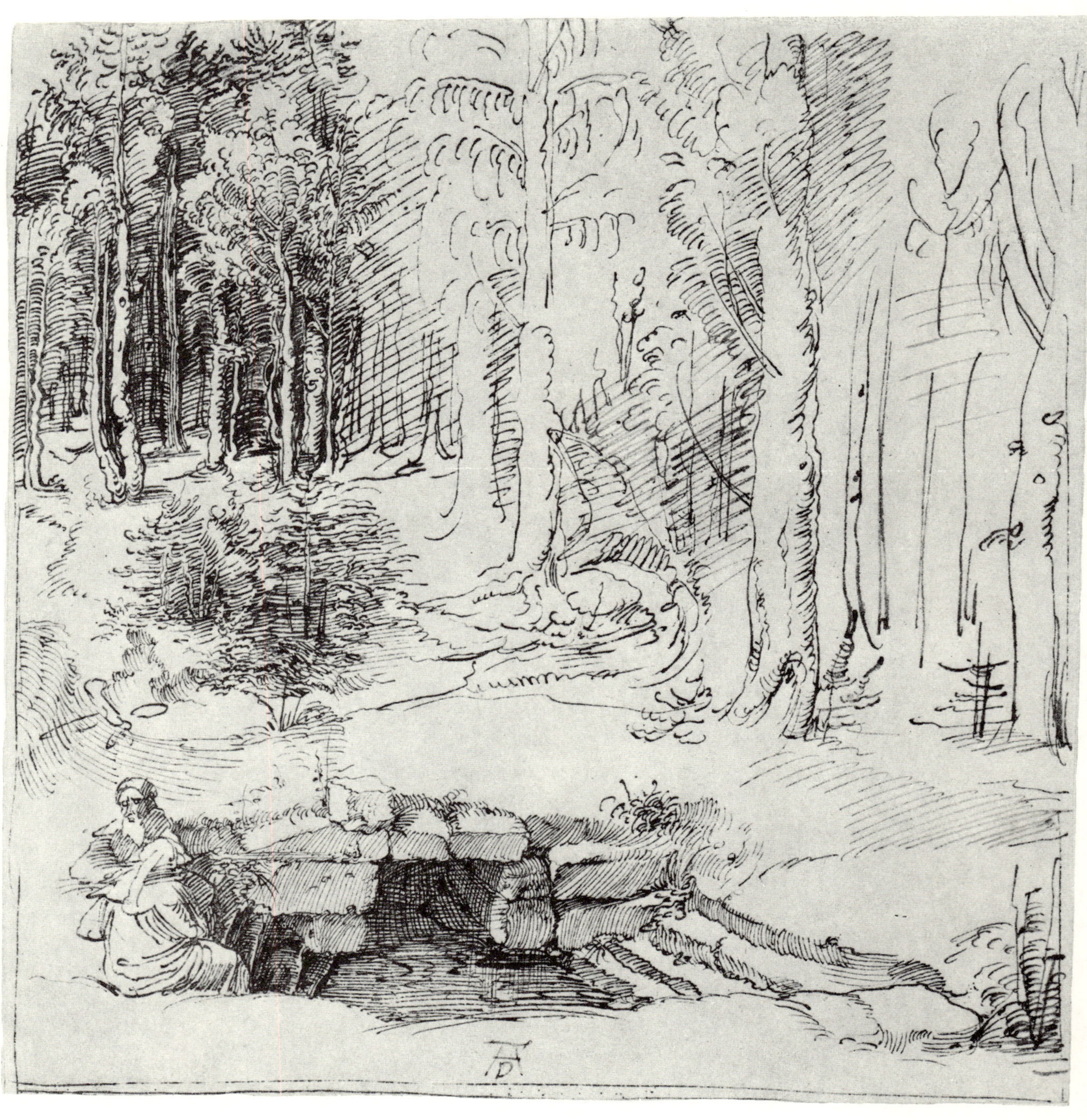

Albrecht Dürer (1471–1528). Forest glade with St. Anthony and St. Paul. Pen and ink; 186 × 186 mm.

OLD MASTER LANDSCAPE DRAWINGS

44 Works

Edited by James Spero

Dover Publications, Inc., New York

PUBLISHER'S NOTE

Although examples can be found in Roman frescoes, and Greek antecedents are known to have existed, it was not until the nineteenth century that the genre of landscape came fully into its own in Western art. Medieval illuminations frequently feature exquisite landscapes, but they are highly stylized and subordinate to the actions being depicted in the foreground. The landscape sketches of Dürer (sometimes regarded as the first "pure" landscapes) and those of da Vinci were probably intended for personal use only, landscape per se lacking appeal to the church and wealthy patrons. Most Italians, especially the Florentines, preferred to devote their endeavors to the human figure. Early in the sixteenth century Northerners such as Altdorfer, Elsheimer, Cranach and Brueghel in particular helped to establish the genre of landscape. Later in the century artists in Rome, notably Claude Lorrain and Poussin, executed impressive landscape canvases, although both artists frequently included a narrative element, drawn from Classical myth or history, in their works. Toward the end of his remarkable career, Rubens developed outstanding landscapes. The eighteenth century saw the vedute of Canaletto and Guardi, the lush works of Watteau and Fragonard, while in England, Gainsborough practiced portraiture because it offered him a living, while landscape, which he actually preferred, did not. Constable and Turner were dominant forces in the nineteenth century, and it was Corot who linked the seventeenth-century landscape tradition with that of the Impressionists, who profoundly raised the art to previously unknown popularity with the general public.

In general, the problems the landscapist must deal with are subtle questions of perspective, the play of atmospheric effects over the landscape and the uses of line and mass. The works included in this selection reveal the manner in which the masters of landscape treated each.

Published in Canada by General Publishing Company, Ltd., 30 Lesmill Road, Don Mills, Toronto, Ontario.
Published in the United Kingdom by Constable and Company, Ltd., 3 The Lanchesters, 162–164 Fulham Palace Road, London W6 9ER.

Old Master Landscape Drawings: 44 Works is a new work, first published by Dover Publications, Inc., in 1992.

Manufactured in the United States of America
Dover Publications, Inc., 31 East 2nd Street, Mineola, N.Y. 11501

Library of Congress Cataloging-in-Publication Data

Old master landscape drawings : 44 works / edited by James Spero.
p. cm.—(Dover art library)
ISBN 0-486-26947-7 (pbk.)
1. Landscape drawing—Catalogs. I. Spero, James. II. Series.
NC790.04 1992 92-19143
743′.936—dc20 CIP

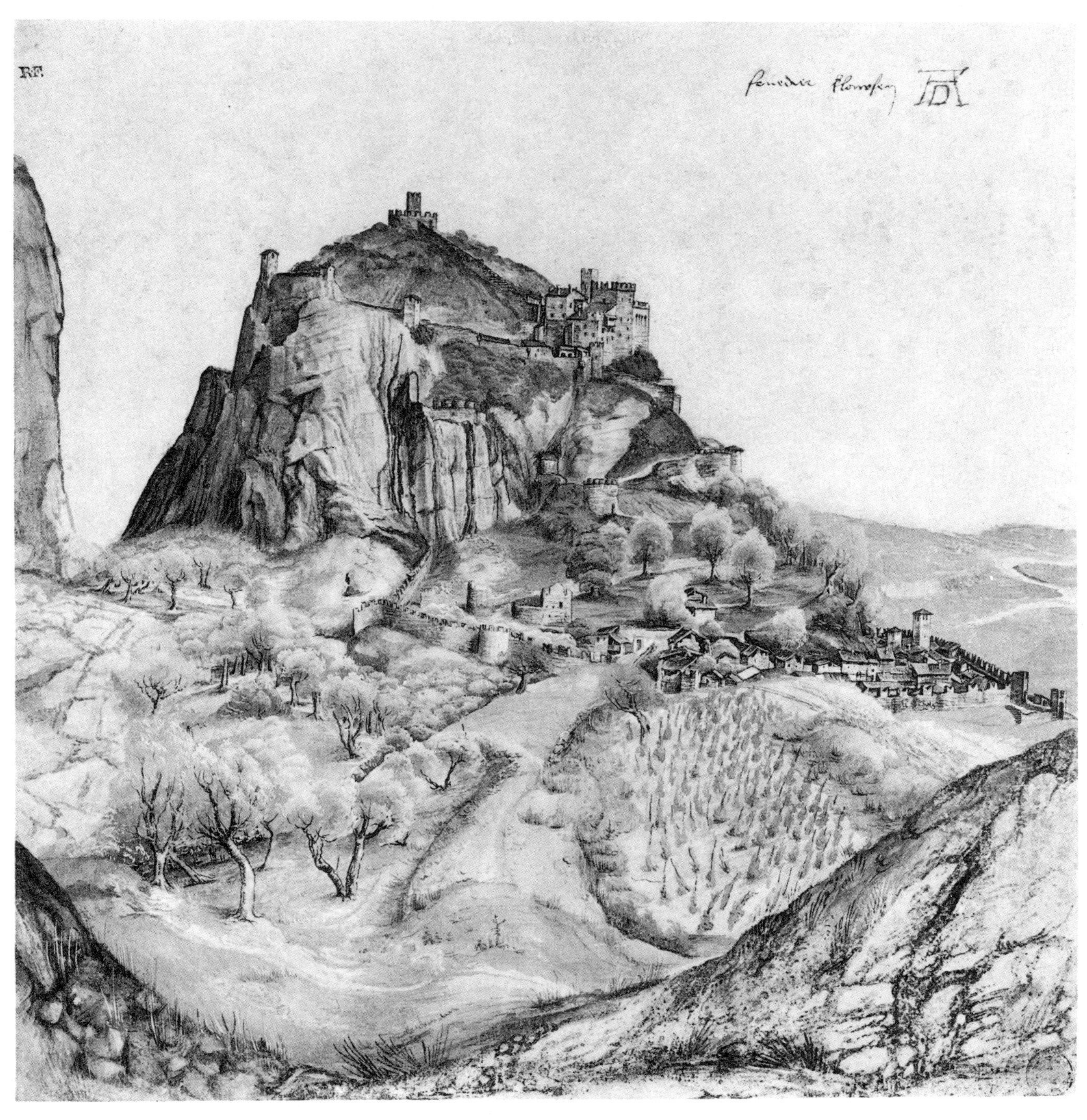

Albrecht Dürer. The citadel of Arco in the South Tyrol. Watercolor over pen; 222 × 221 mm.

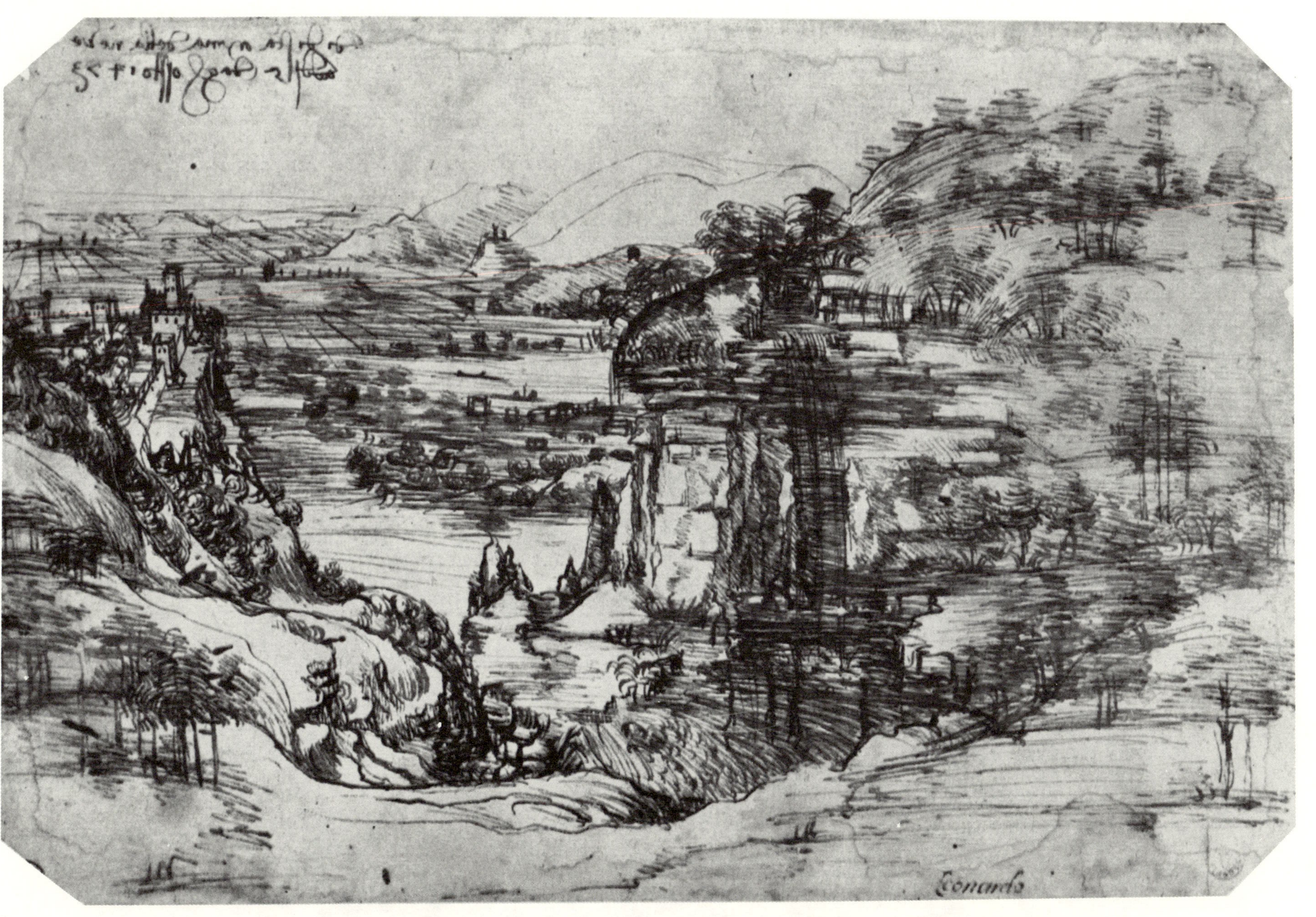

Leonardo da Vinci (1452–1519). The Valley of the Arno, near Florence. Pen and ink; 193 × 285 mm.

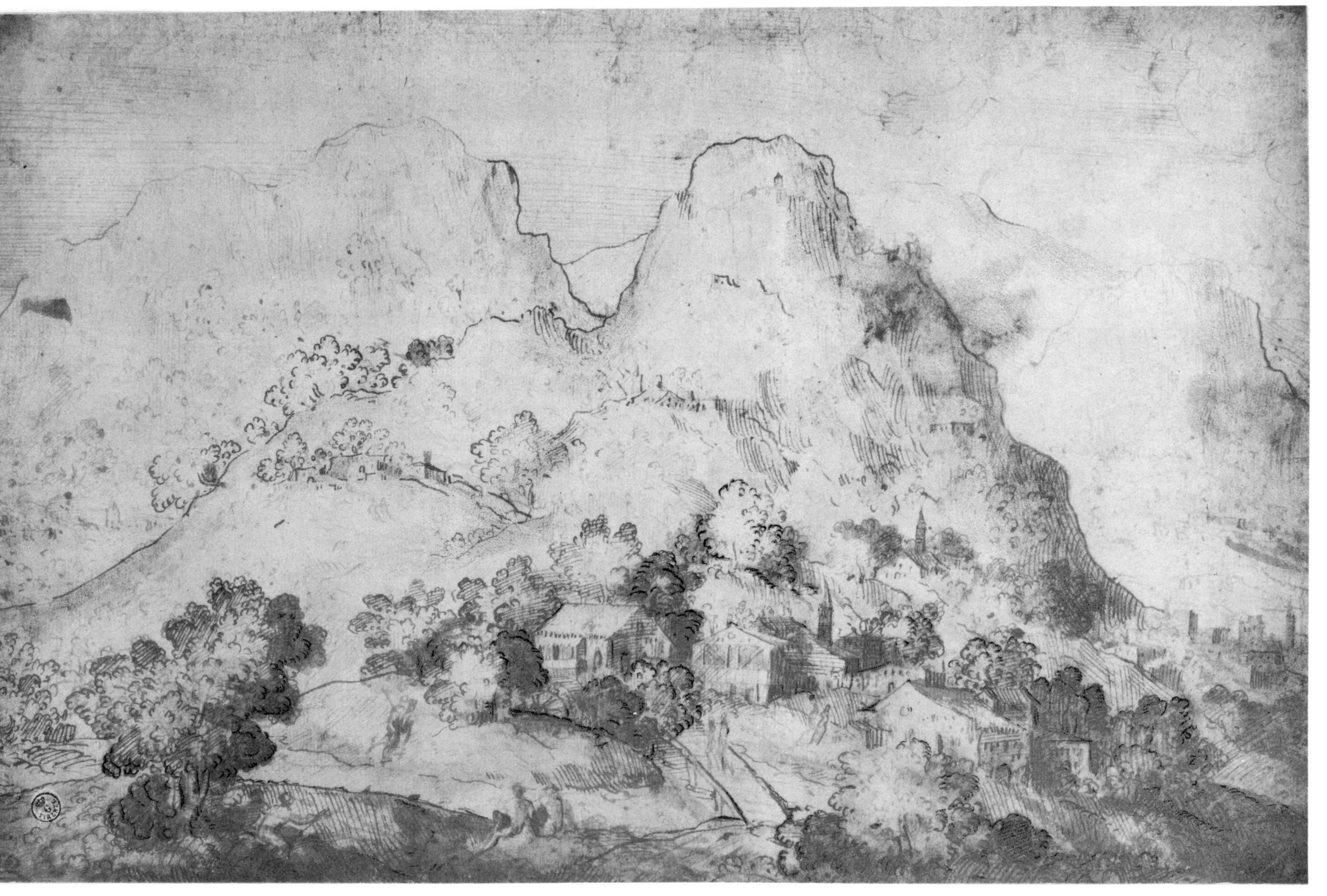

Dosso Dossi (Giovanni Lutero; 1479/90–1542). Mountain landscape. Pen and bister; 252 × 278 mm.

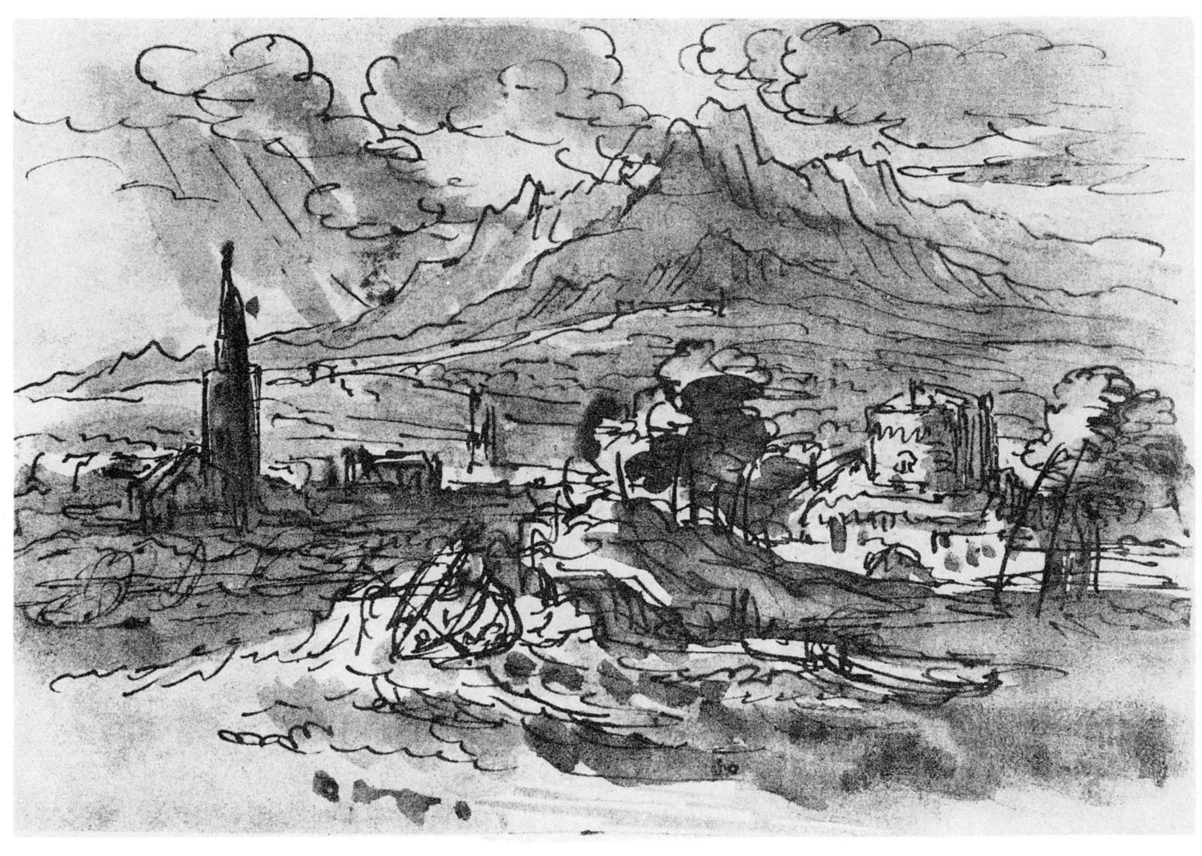

Titian (Tiziano Vecellio; ca. 1485 or 1488/89–1576). Landscape of the foothills of the Alps. Pen and ink with wash; 114 × 163 mm.

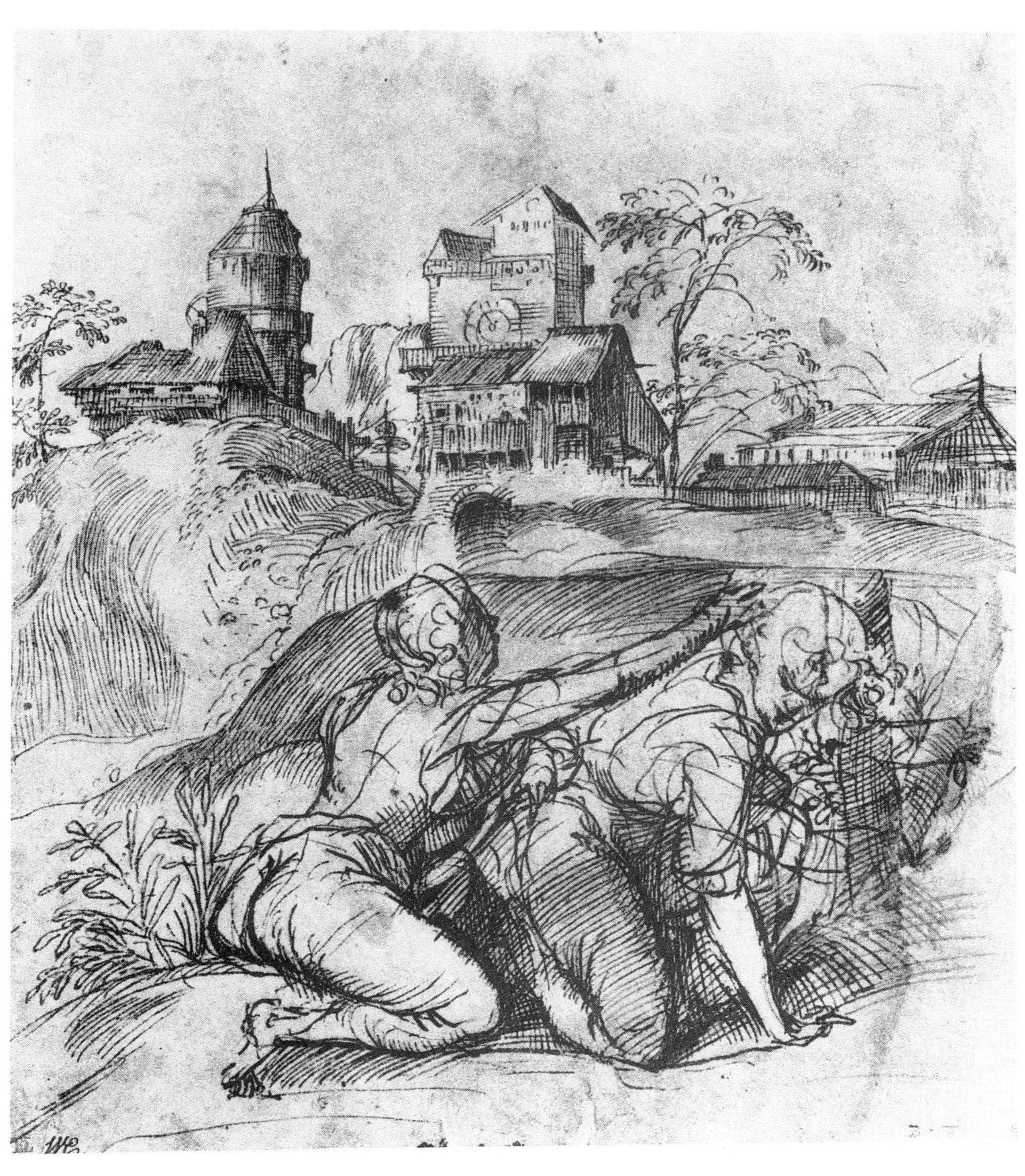

Titian. Two youths in a landscape. Pen and ink; 235 × 212 mm.

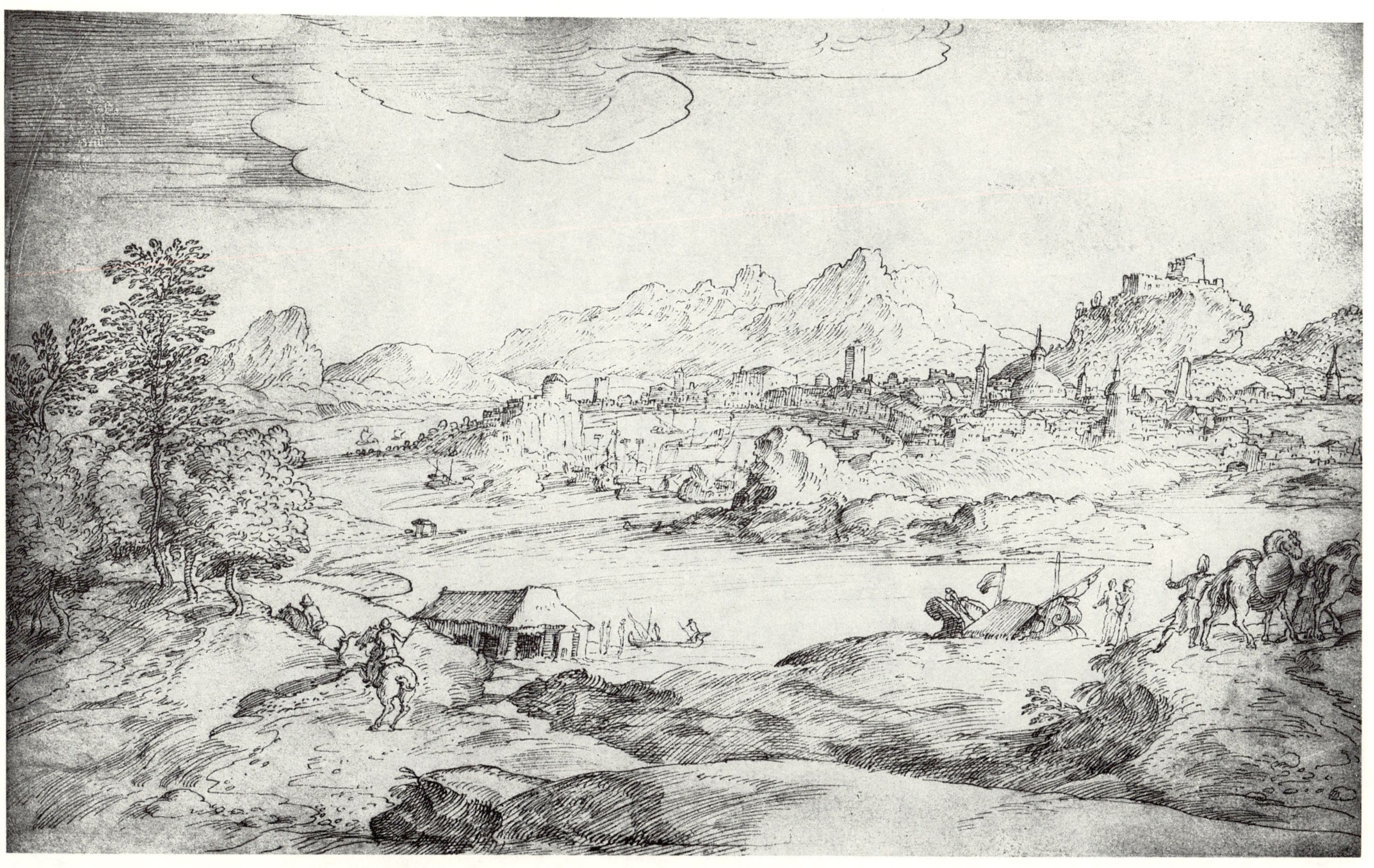

Domenico Campagnola (ca. 1484–ca. 1563). Landscape. Pen and bister.

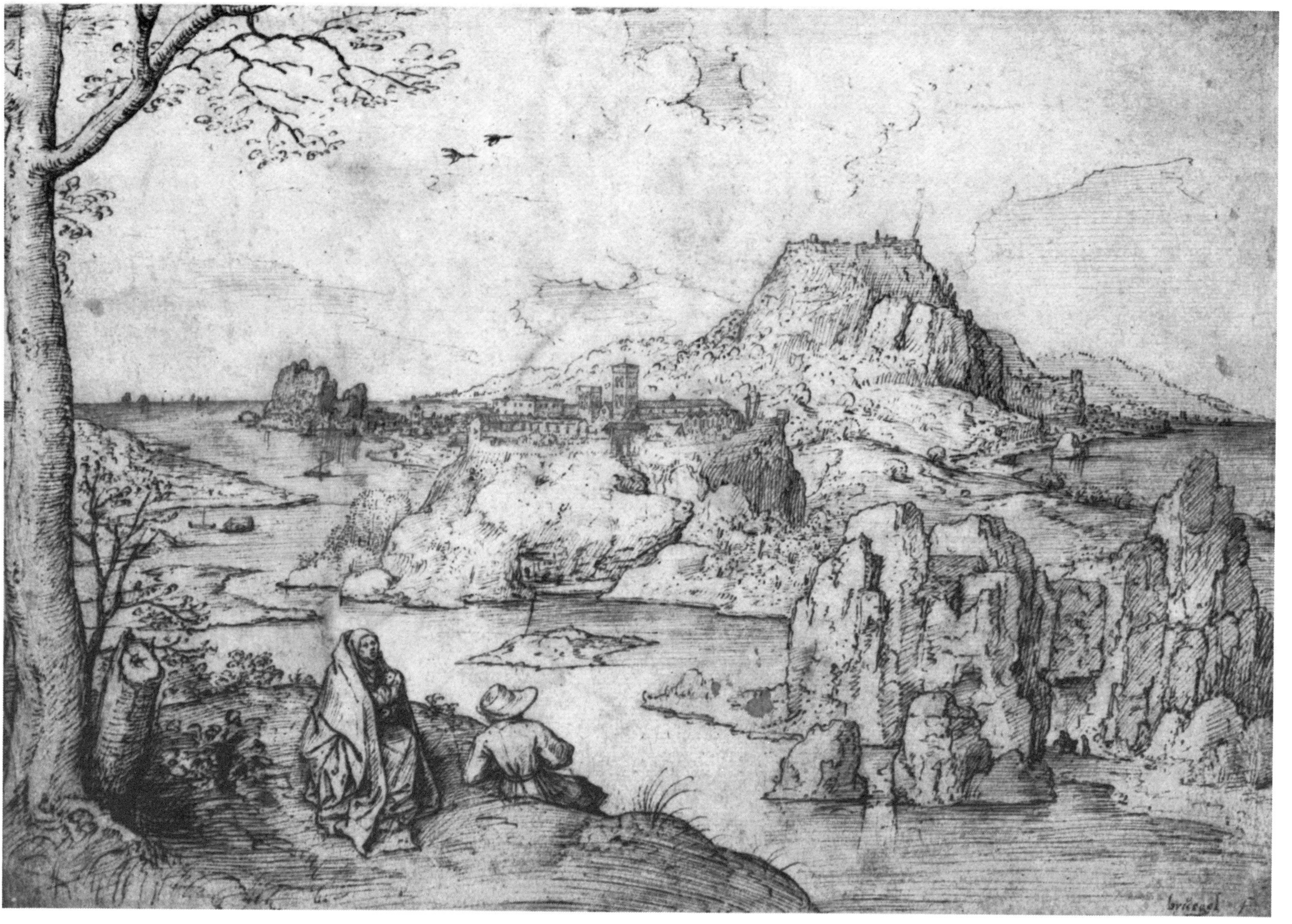

Pieter Brueghel the Elder (ca. 1525–1569). Landscape with Rest on the Flight to Egypt. Pen and brown ink: 203 × 282 mm.

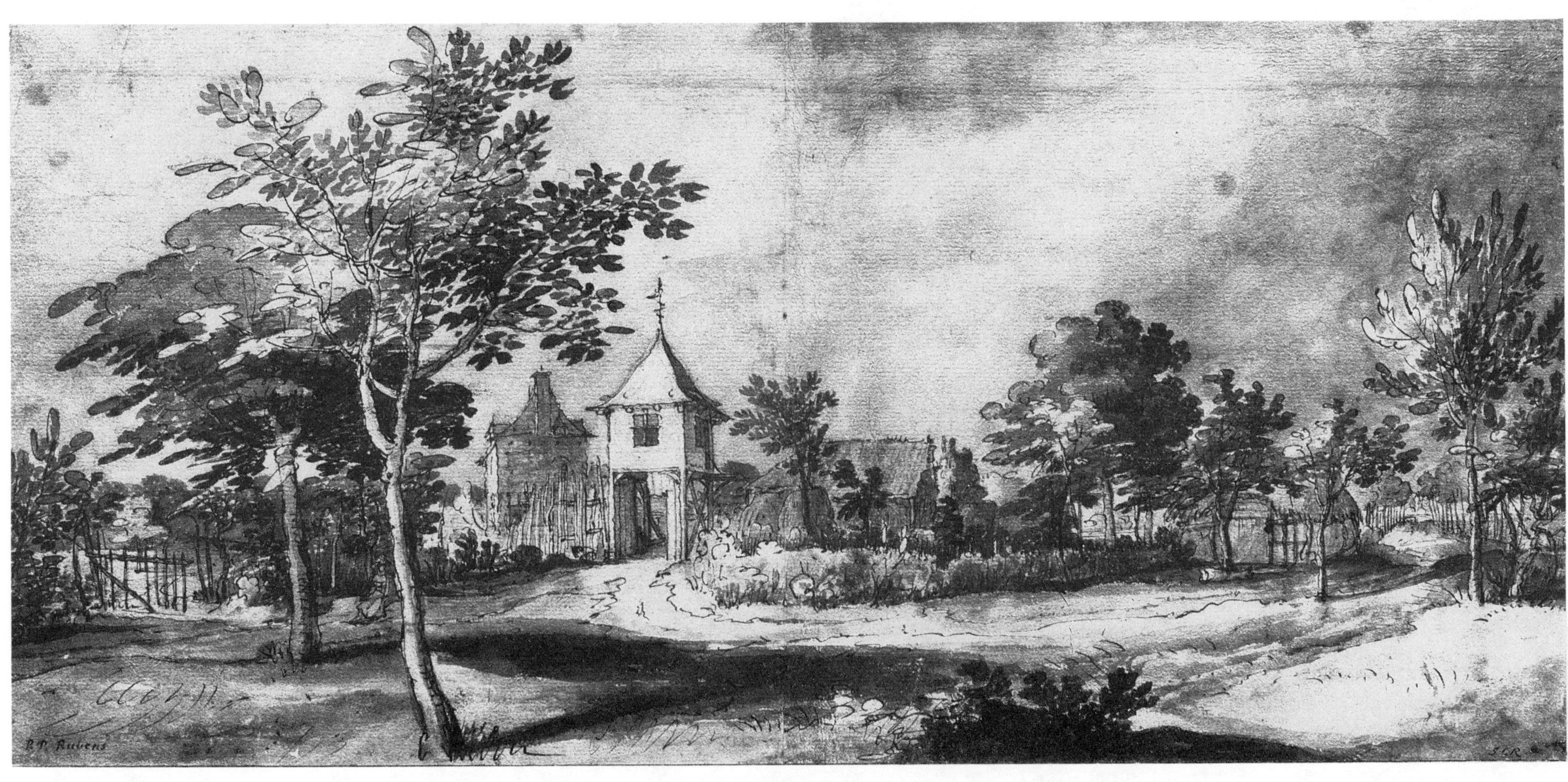

Peter Paul Rubens (1577–1640). Landscape with entrance to a farm. Pen and bister washed with color.

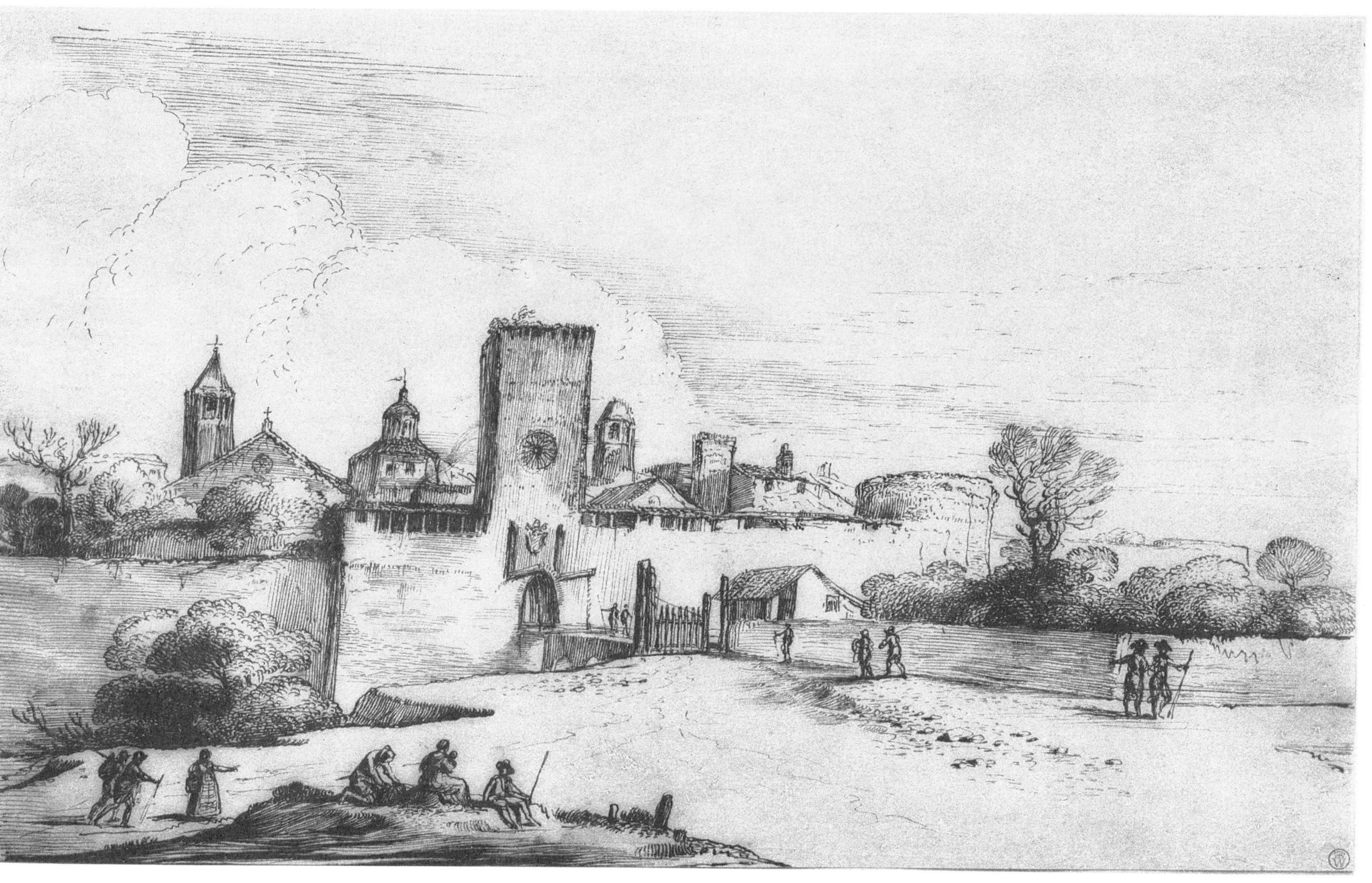

Guercino (Giovanni Francesco Barbieri; 1591–1666). View of a walled town with a tower and drawbridge. Pen and bister, washed.

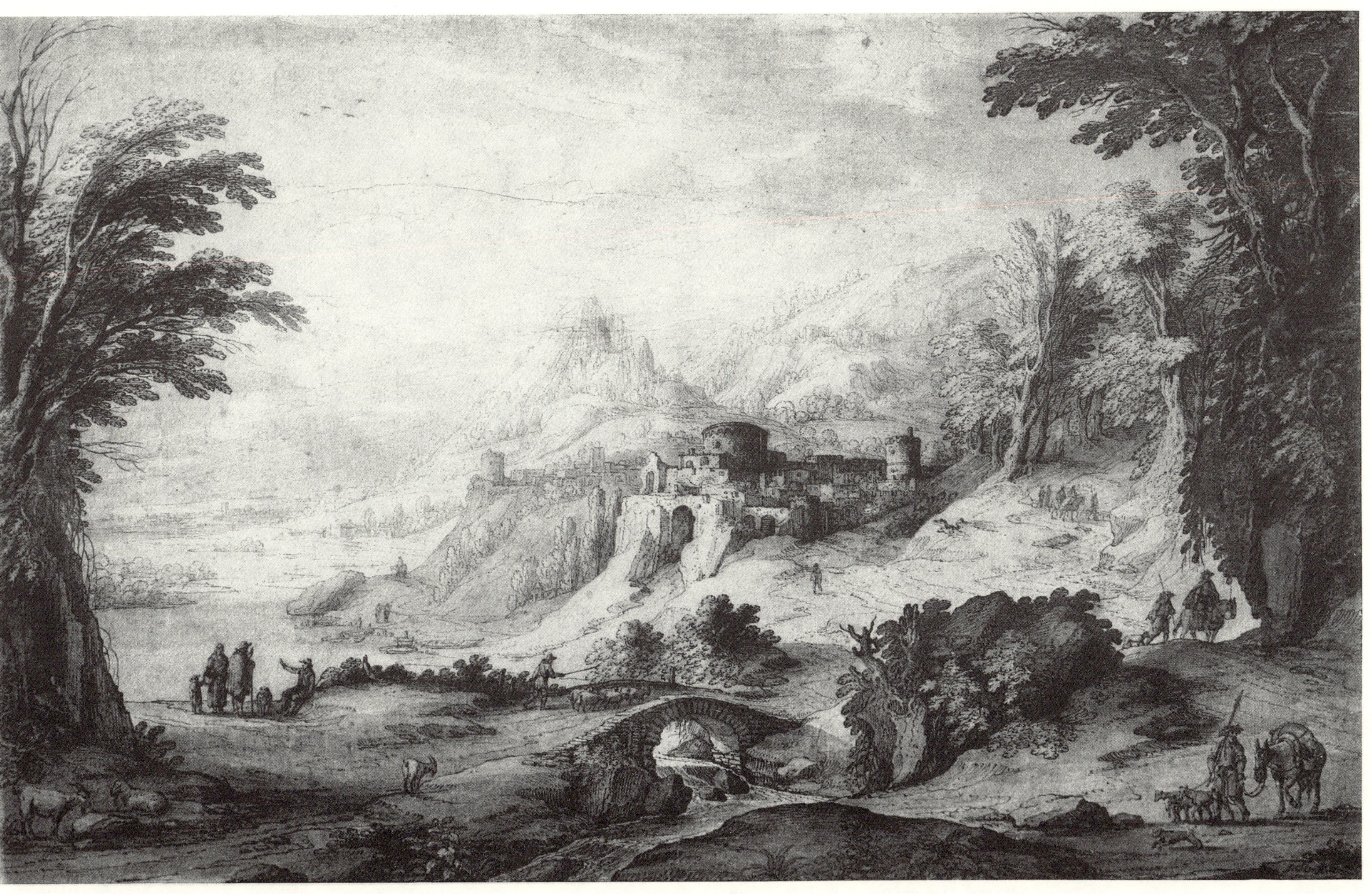

Paul Brill (1554–1626). Mountain landscape. Pen and bister wash.

Jacques Callot (1592/93–1635). Alpine landscape with river. Pen and ink; 220 × 305 mm.

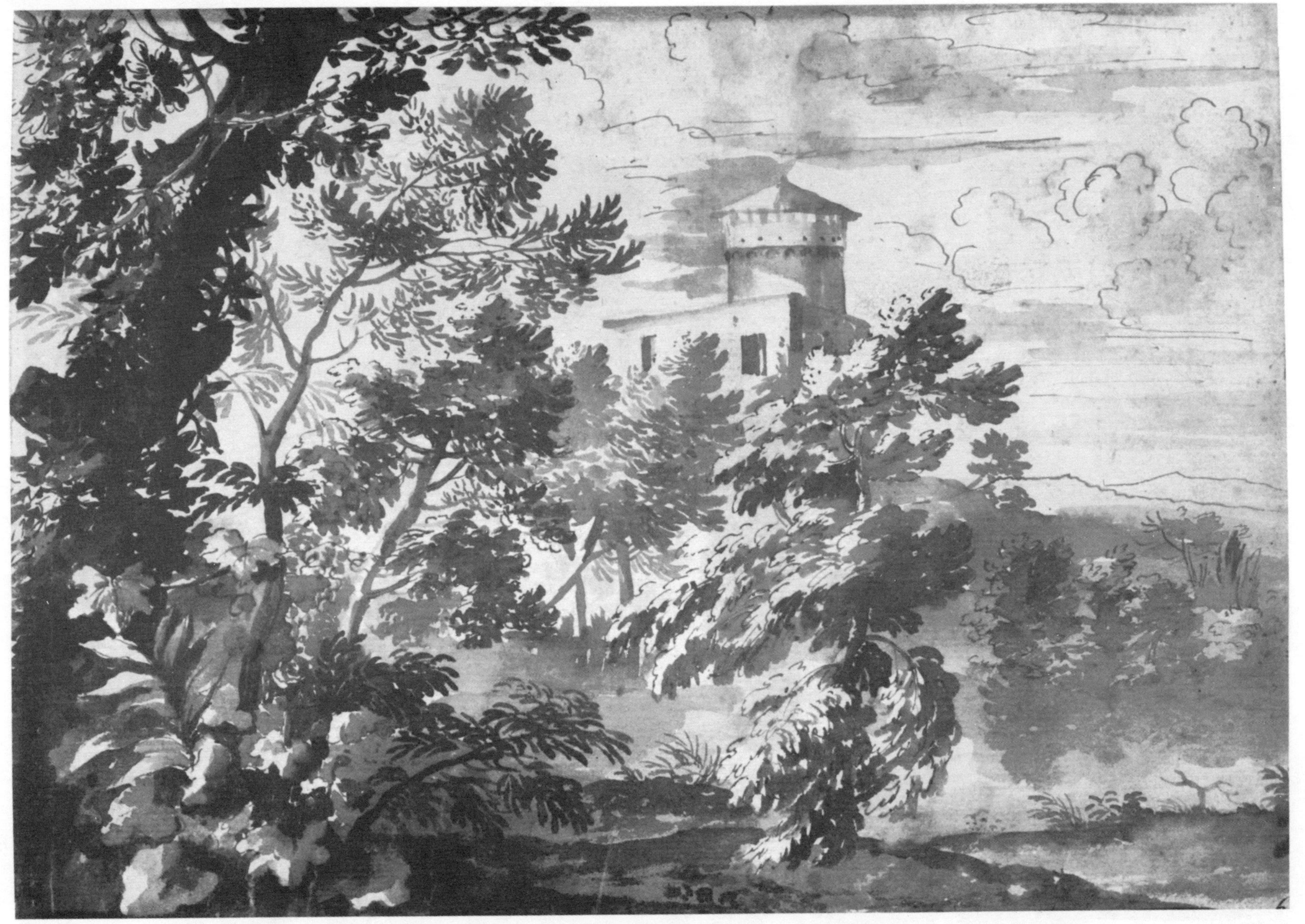

Nicolas Poussin (1594–1665). Landscape with trees and a tower. Pen and bister wash; 194 × 267 mm.

Anthony Van Dyck (1599–1641). A wooded landscape. Watercolor.

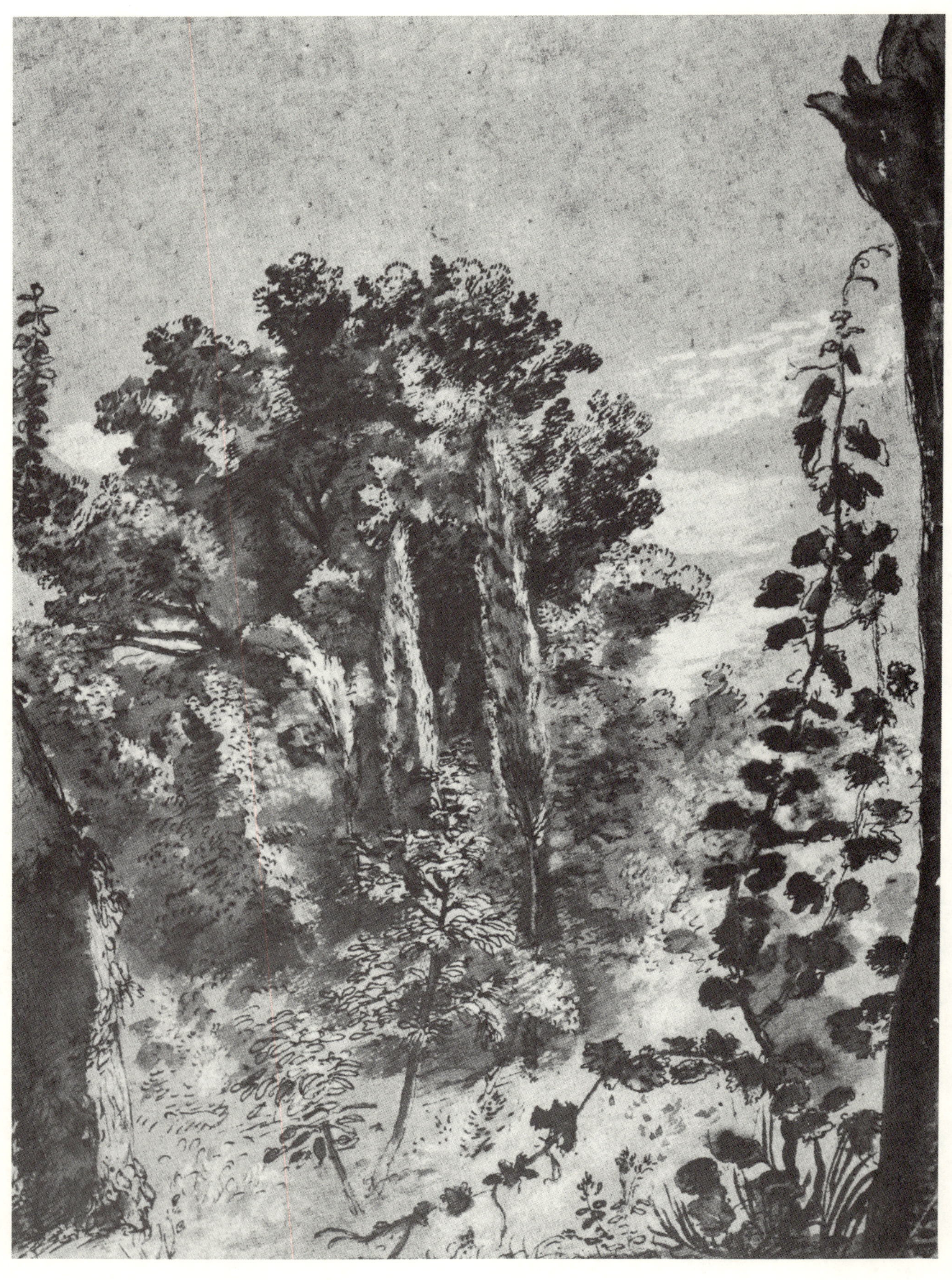

Claude Lorrain (Gellée; 1600–1682). Trees and vine. Pen and bister wash on blue paper; 275 × 210 mm.

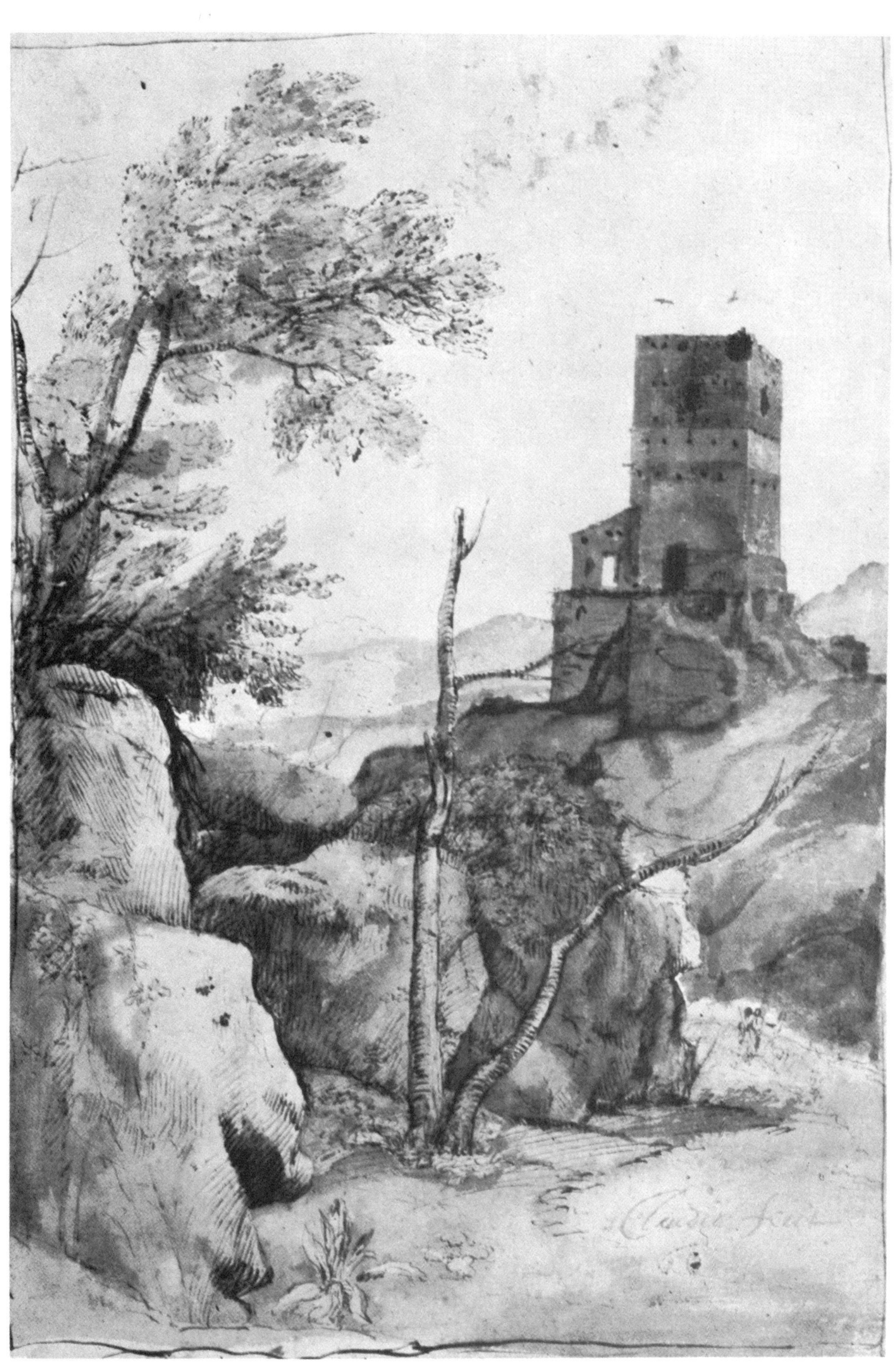

Claude Lorrain. Campagna landscape. Pen, bister and wash; 320 × 215 mm.

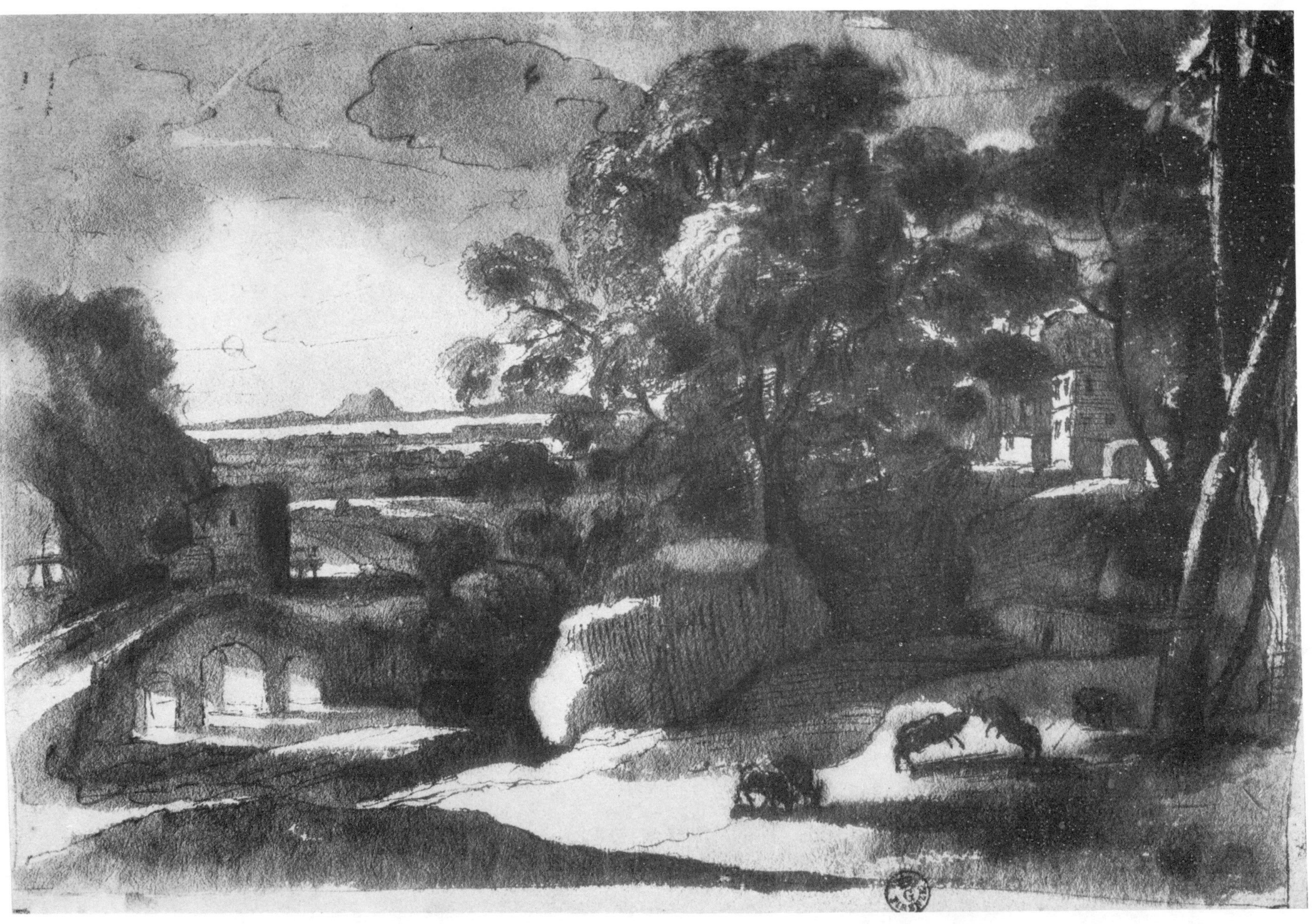

Claude Lorrain. Landscape with goats. Pen and bister; 175 × 245 mm.

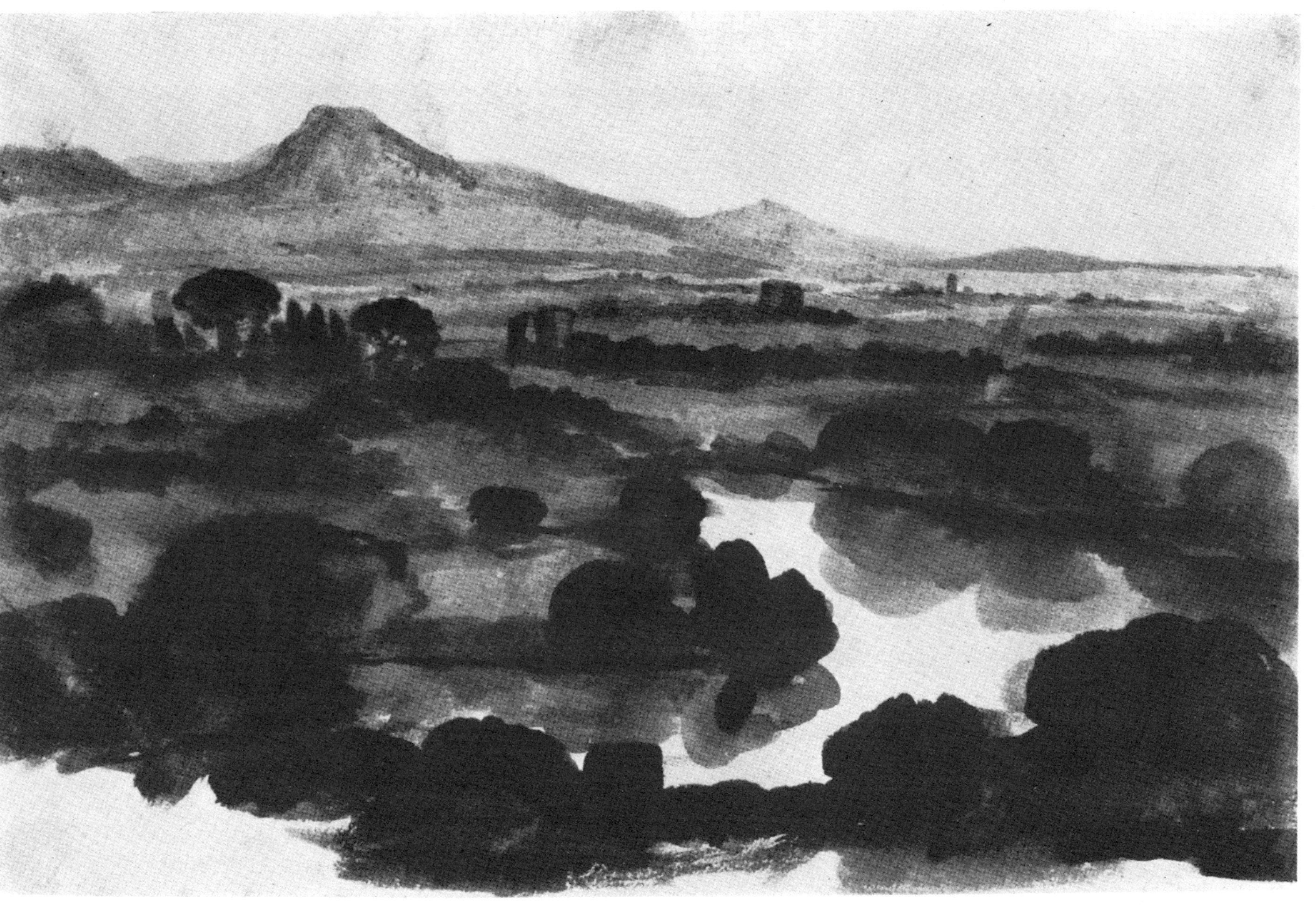

Claude Lorrain. The Tiber above Rome. Brush and bister wash; 188 × 270 mm.

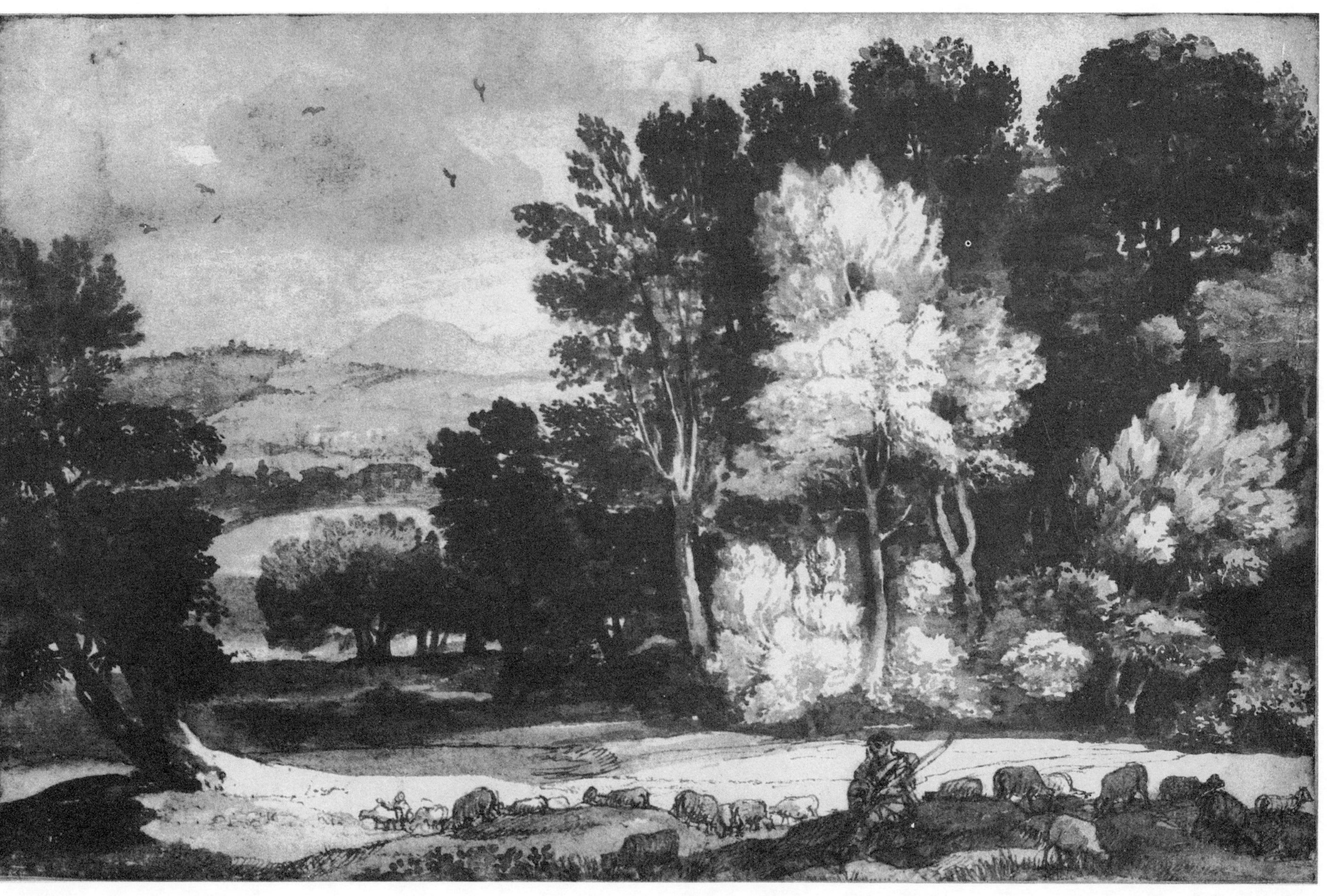

Claude Lorrain. Landscape: the edge of a wood. Pen and bister, washed.

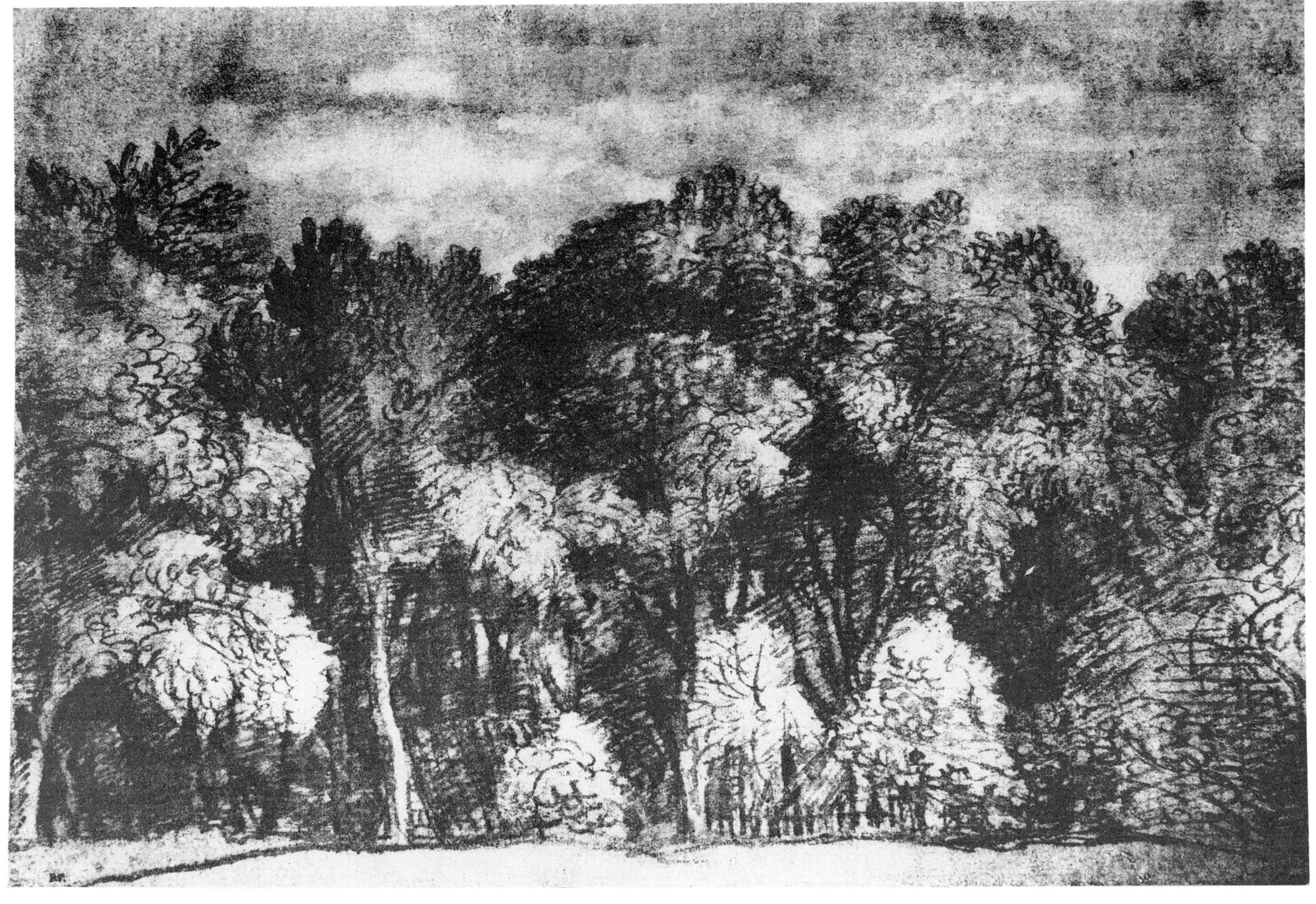

Rembrandt (Harmenszoon van Rijn; 1606–1669). Wooded landscape.

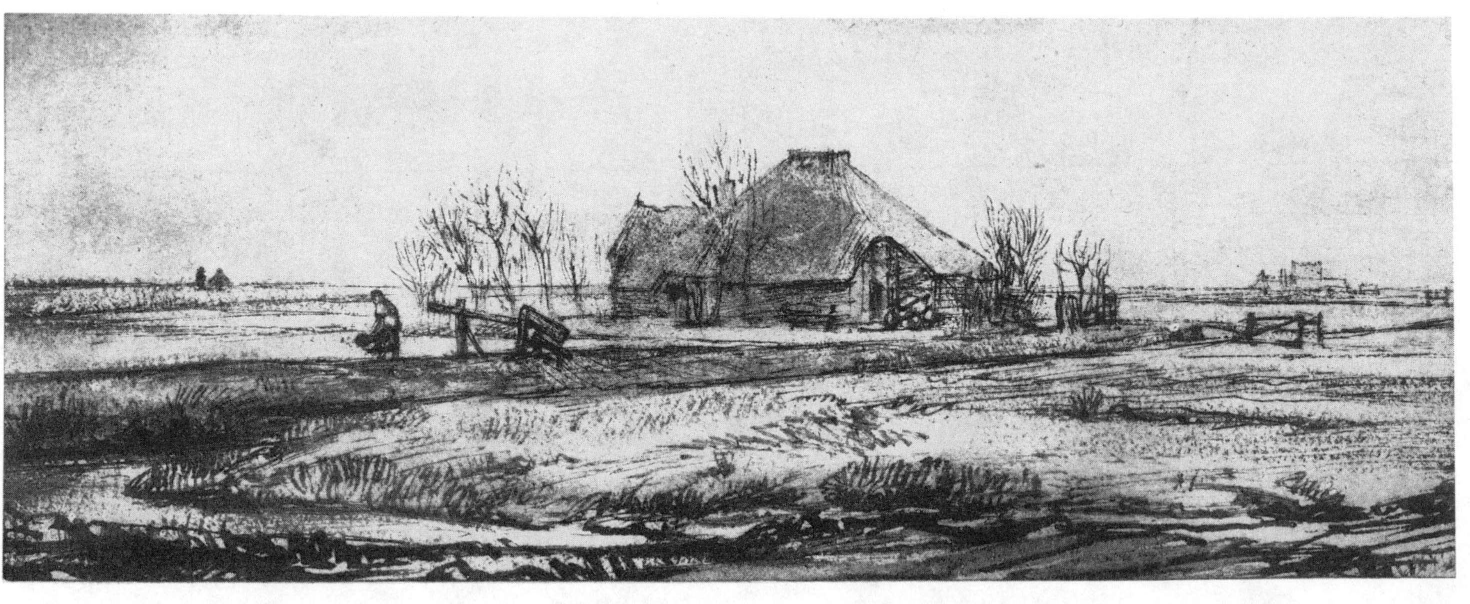

Rembrandt. Landscape with a thatched cottage. Pen and bister wash with white body color; 76 × 190 mm.

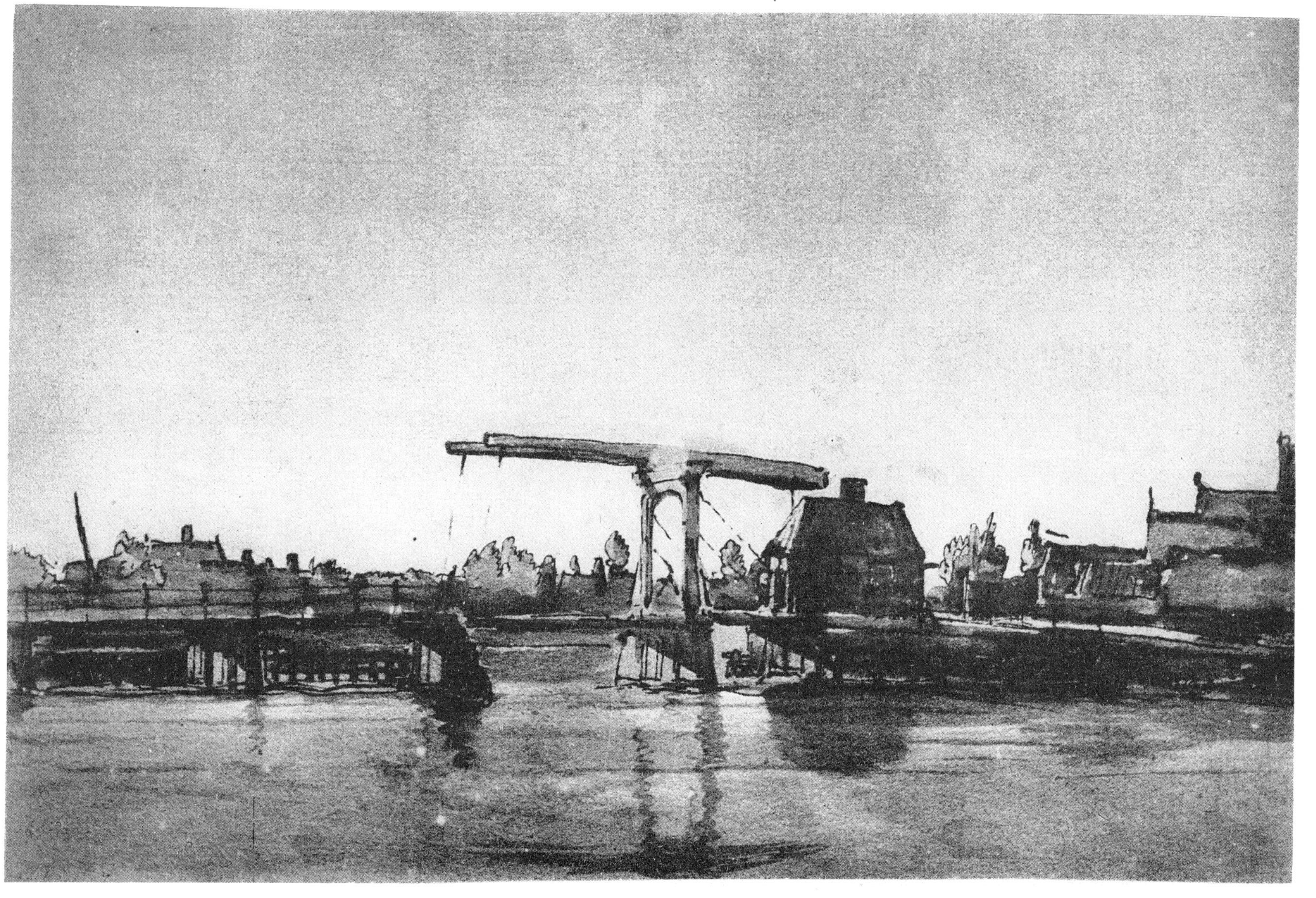

Rembrandt. Landscape with bridge.

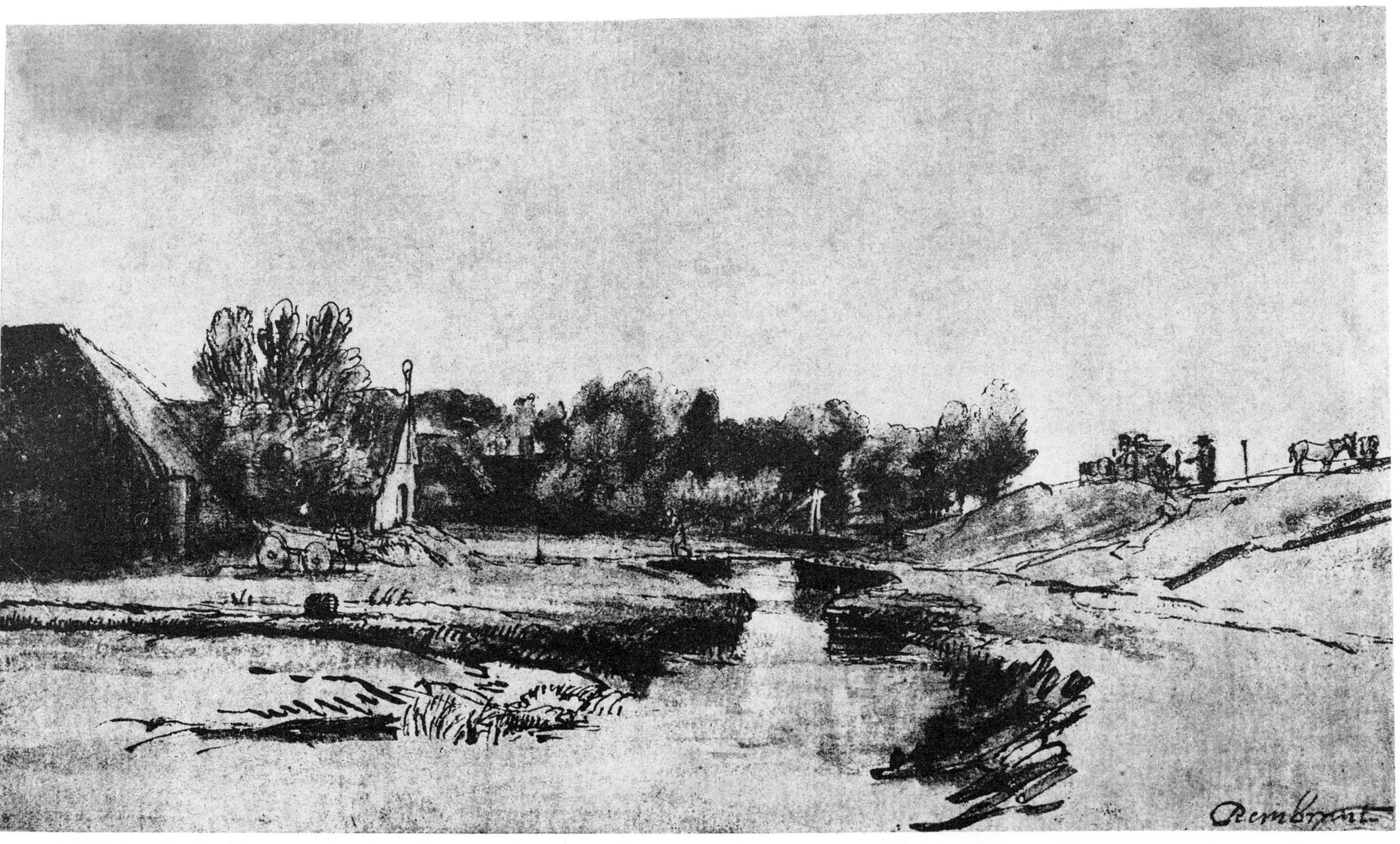

Rembrandt. Farm building at the "Dijk." Pen and bister with bister and India ink wash; 143 × 242 mm.

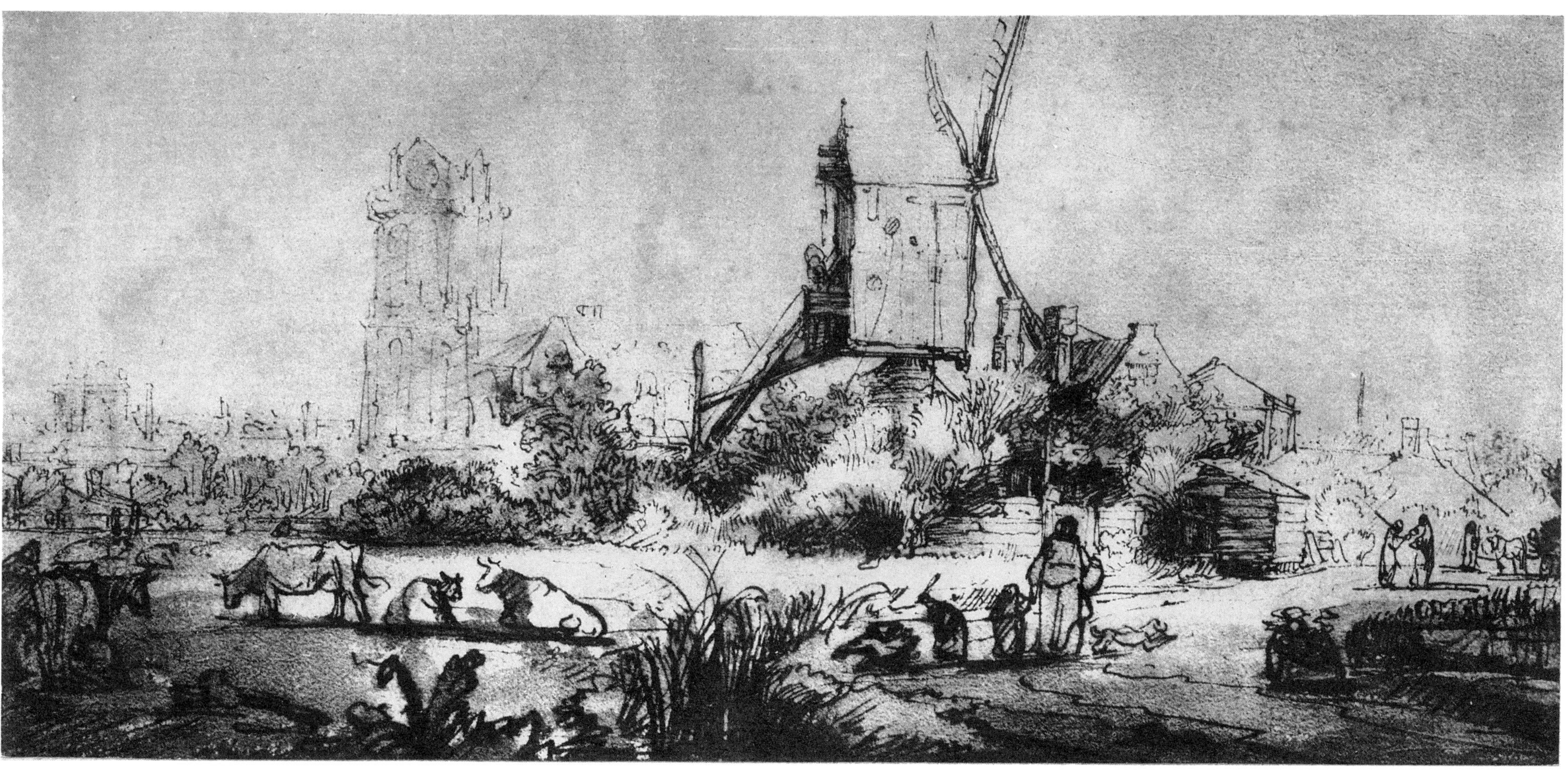

Rembrandt. Landscape with windmill.

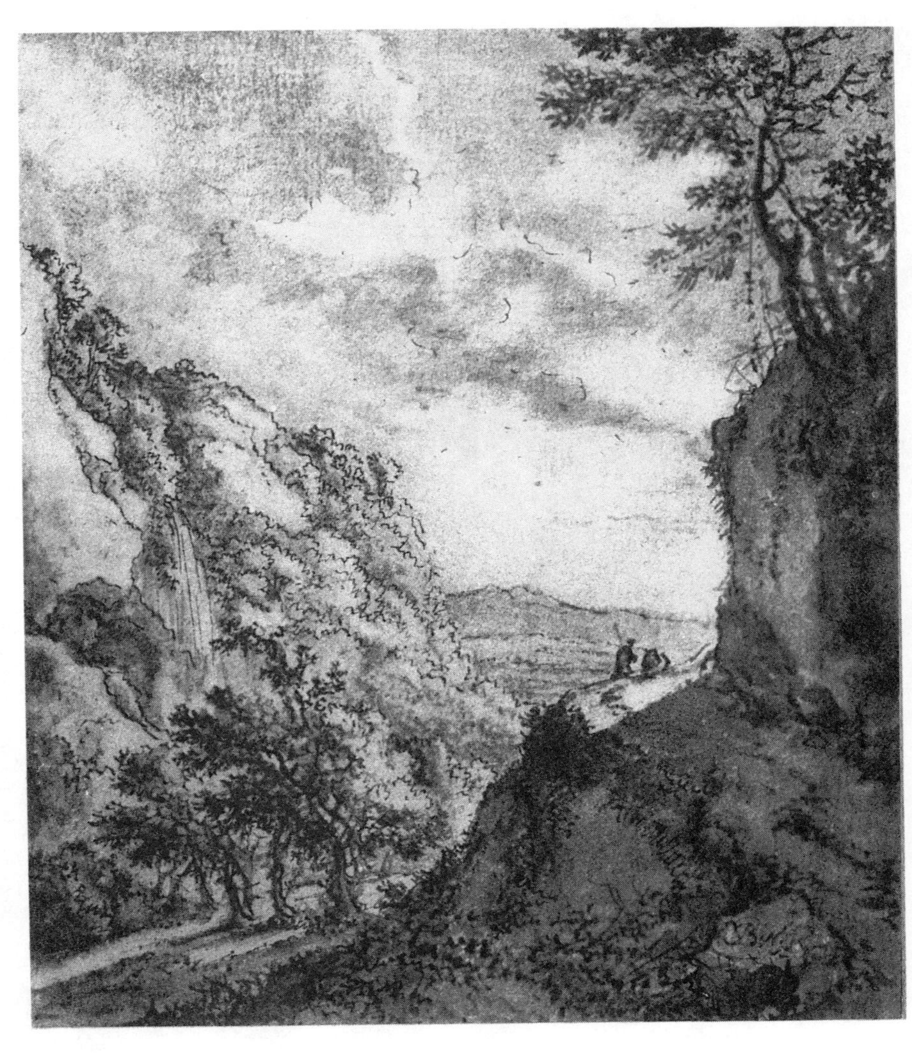

Jan Both (1610–1652). Landscape.

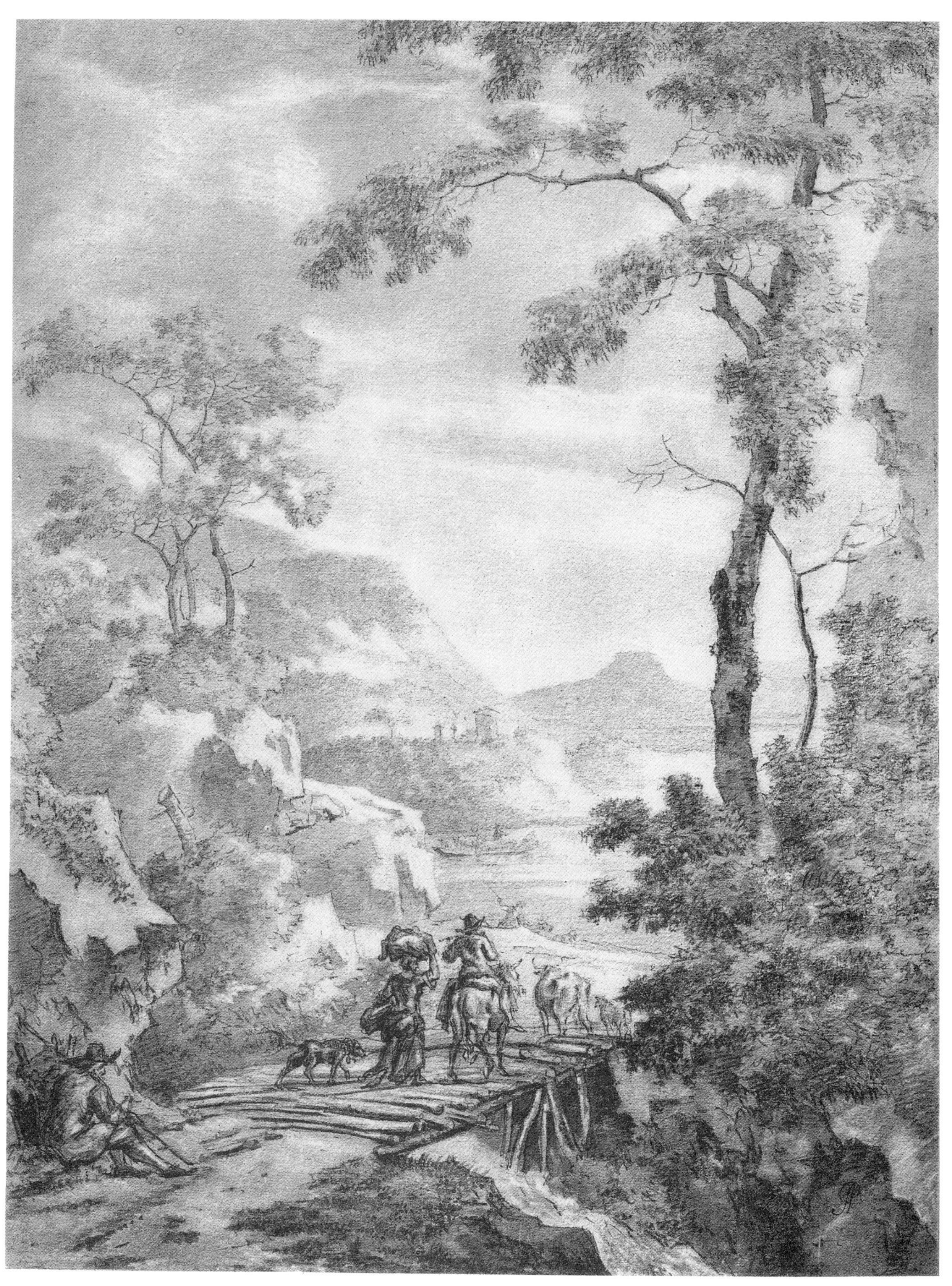

Adam Pynaker (1622–1673). Landscape.

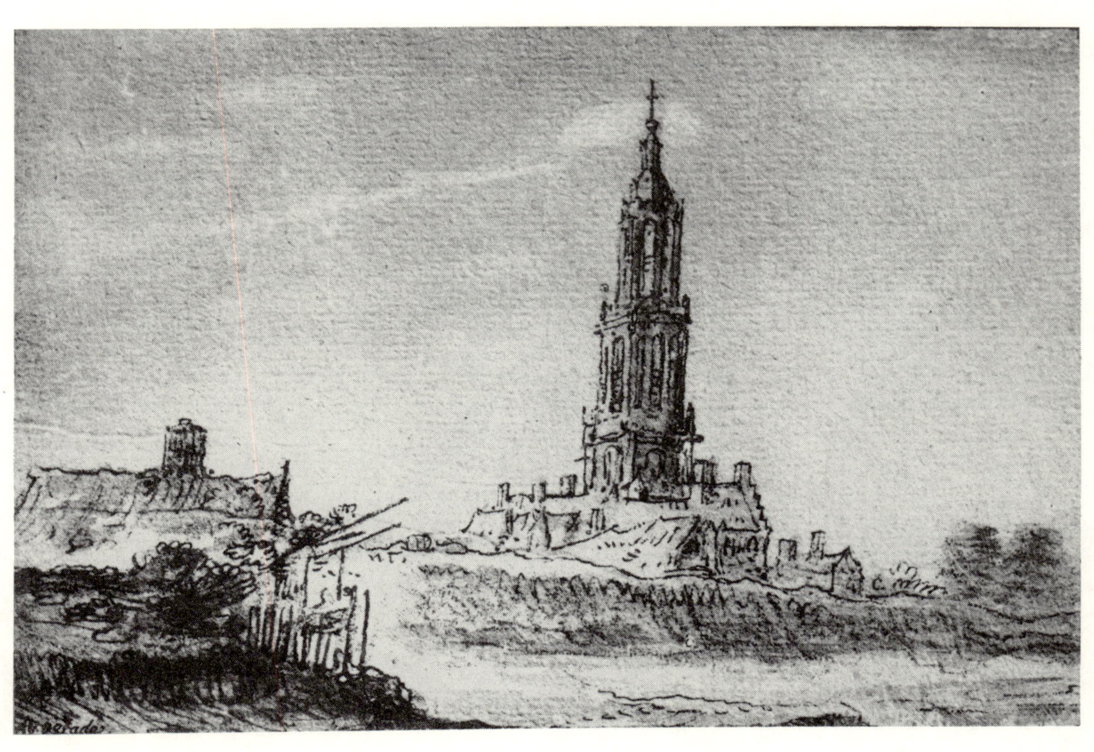

Adriaen van Ostade (1610–1685). Landscape with church.

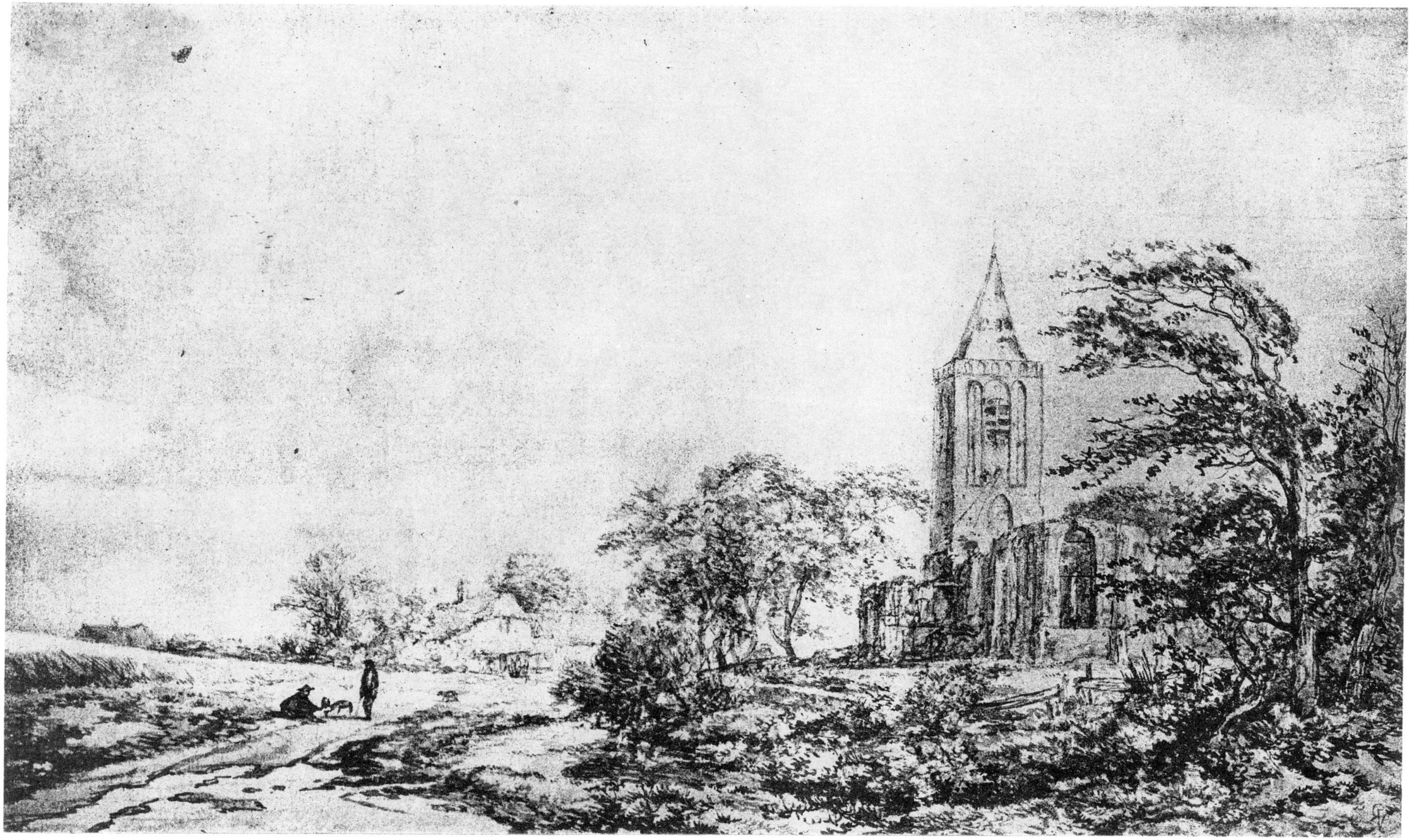

Jacob van Ruisdael (1628–1682). Landscape with ruined church.

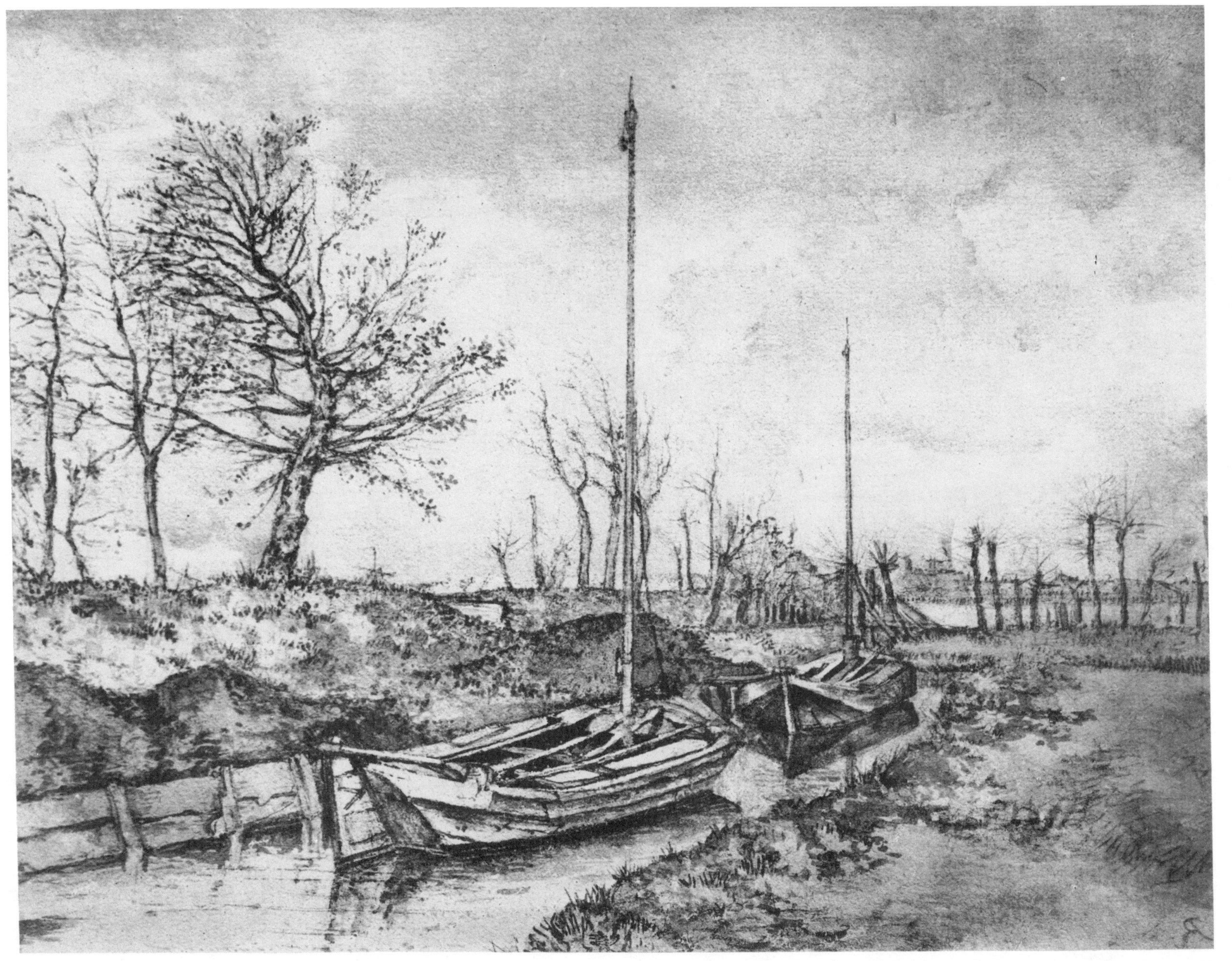

Jacob van Ruisdael. Landscape with canal and boats.

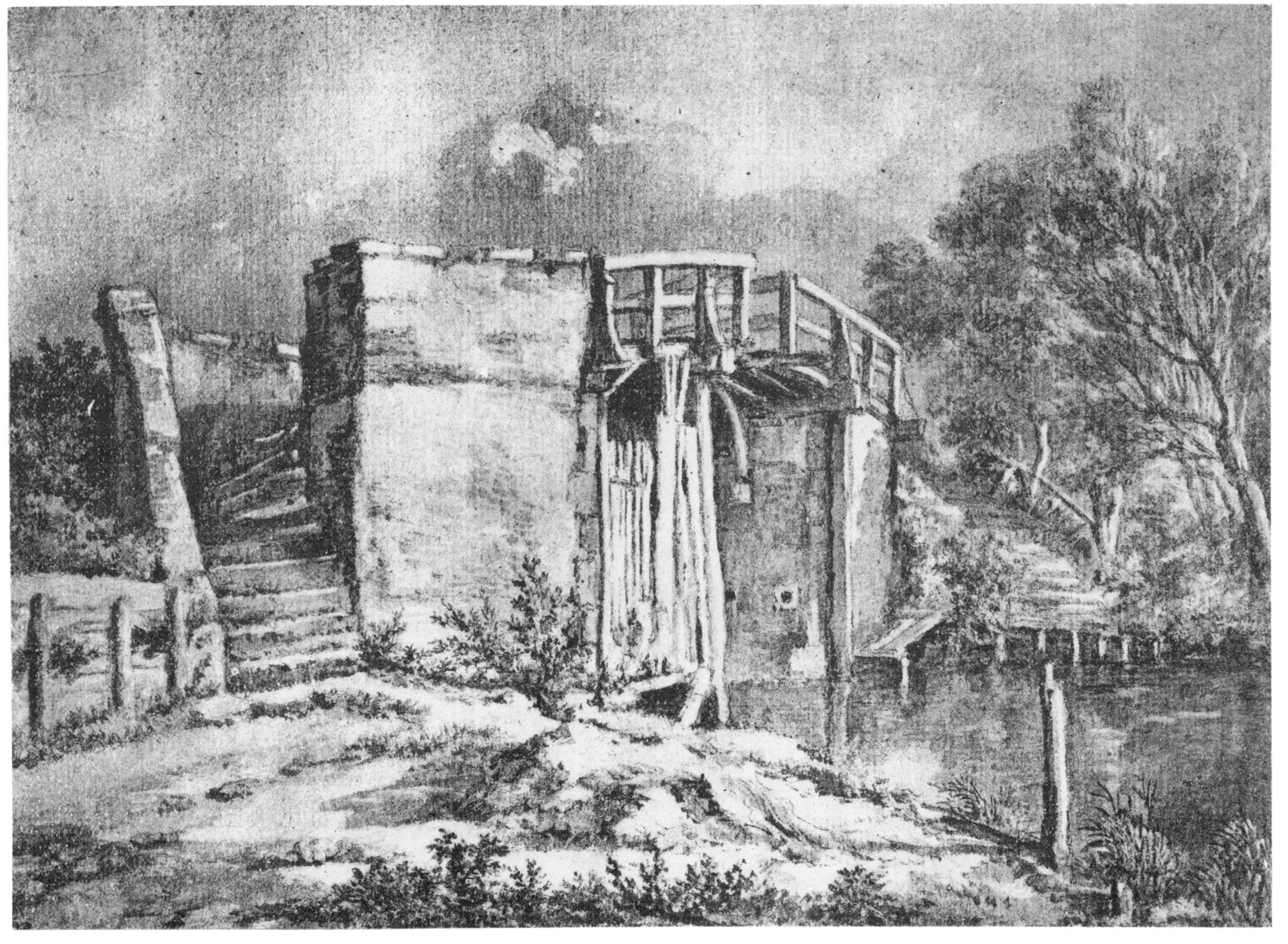

Jacob van Ruisdael. Landscape with bridge.

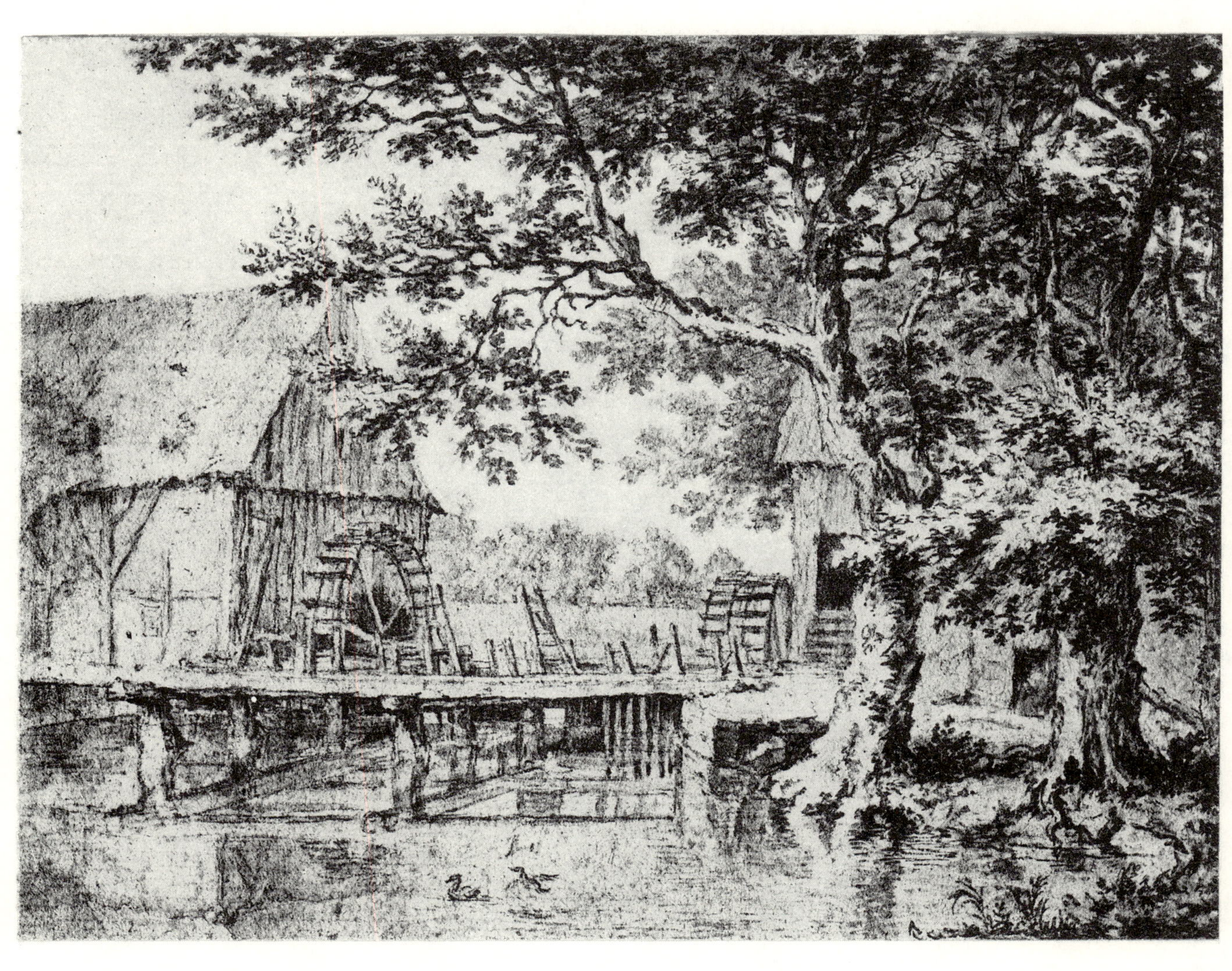

Jacob van Ruisdael. Landscape with mills.

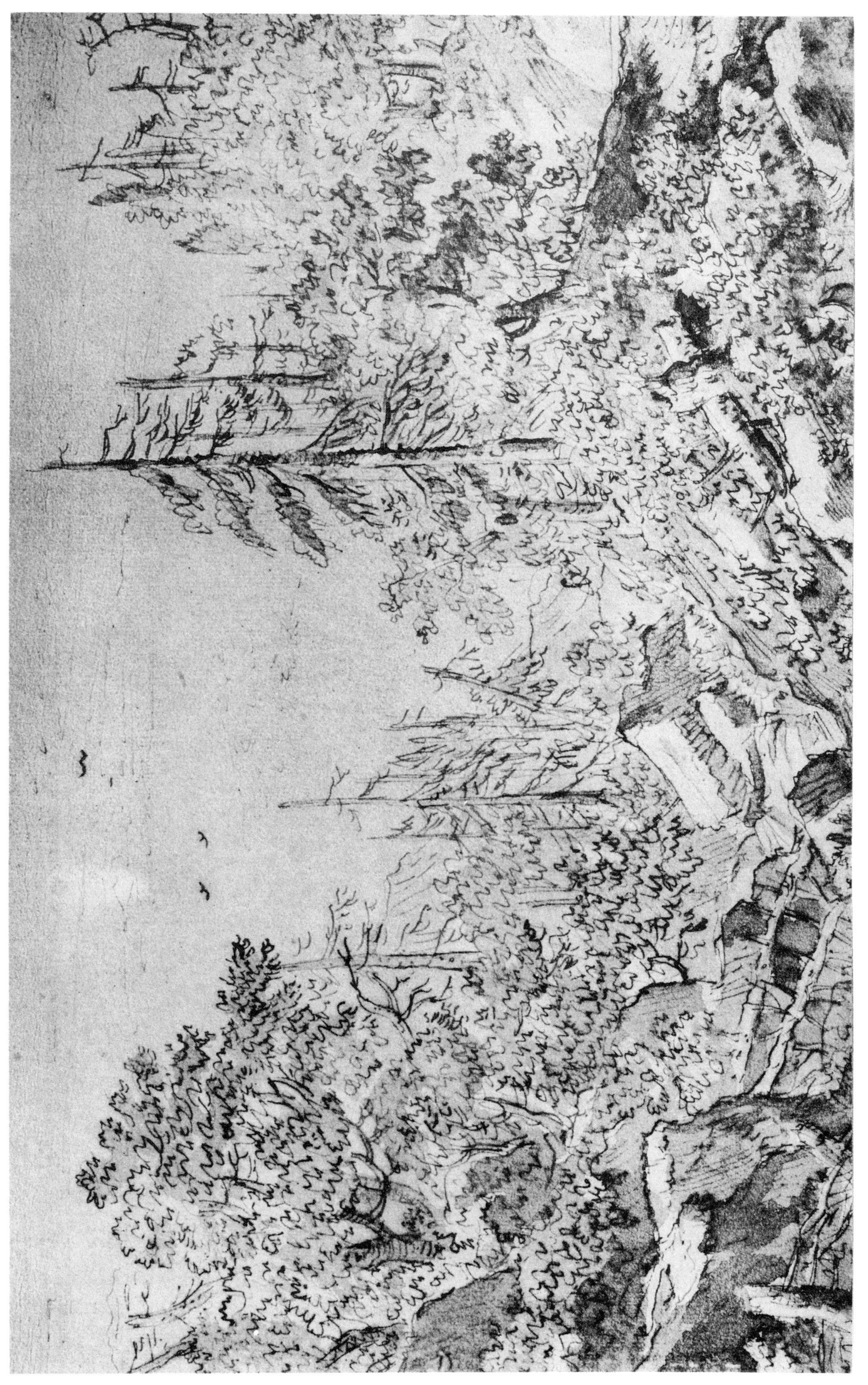

Jan Hackaert (1629–1699?). Wooded landscape.

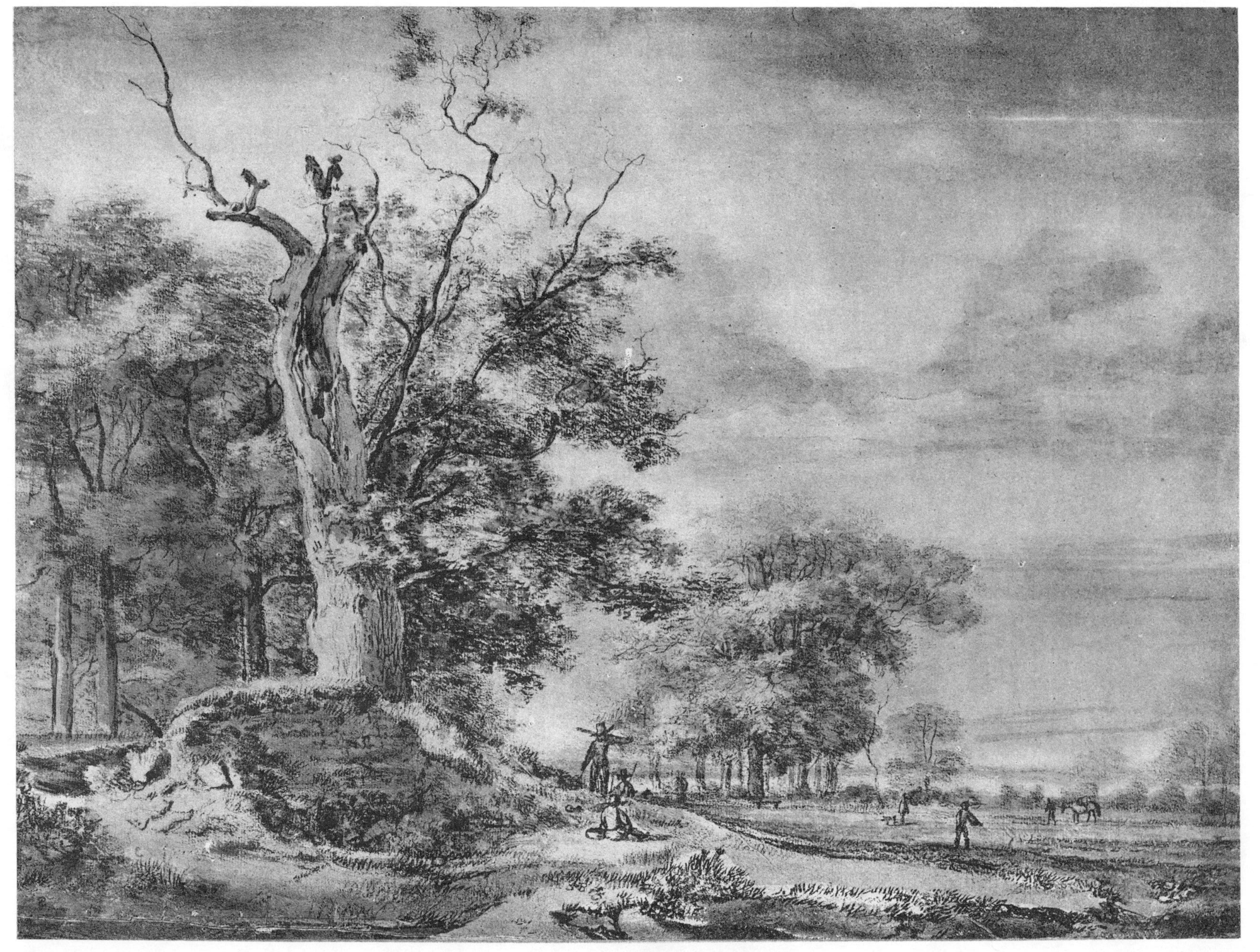

Meindert Hobbema (1638–1709). Landscape.

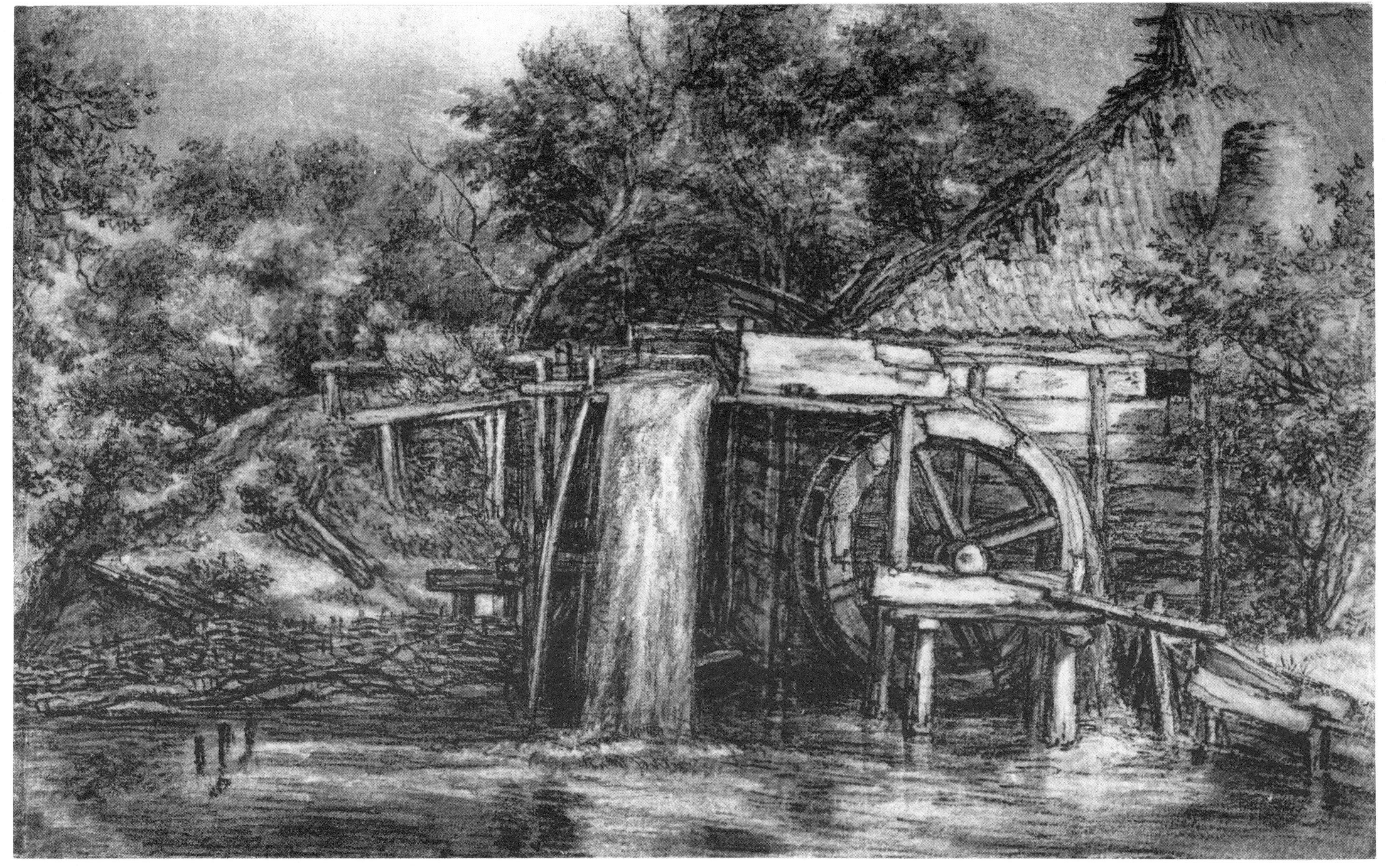

Meindert Hobbema. Landscape with mill.

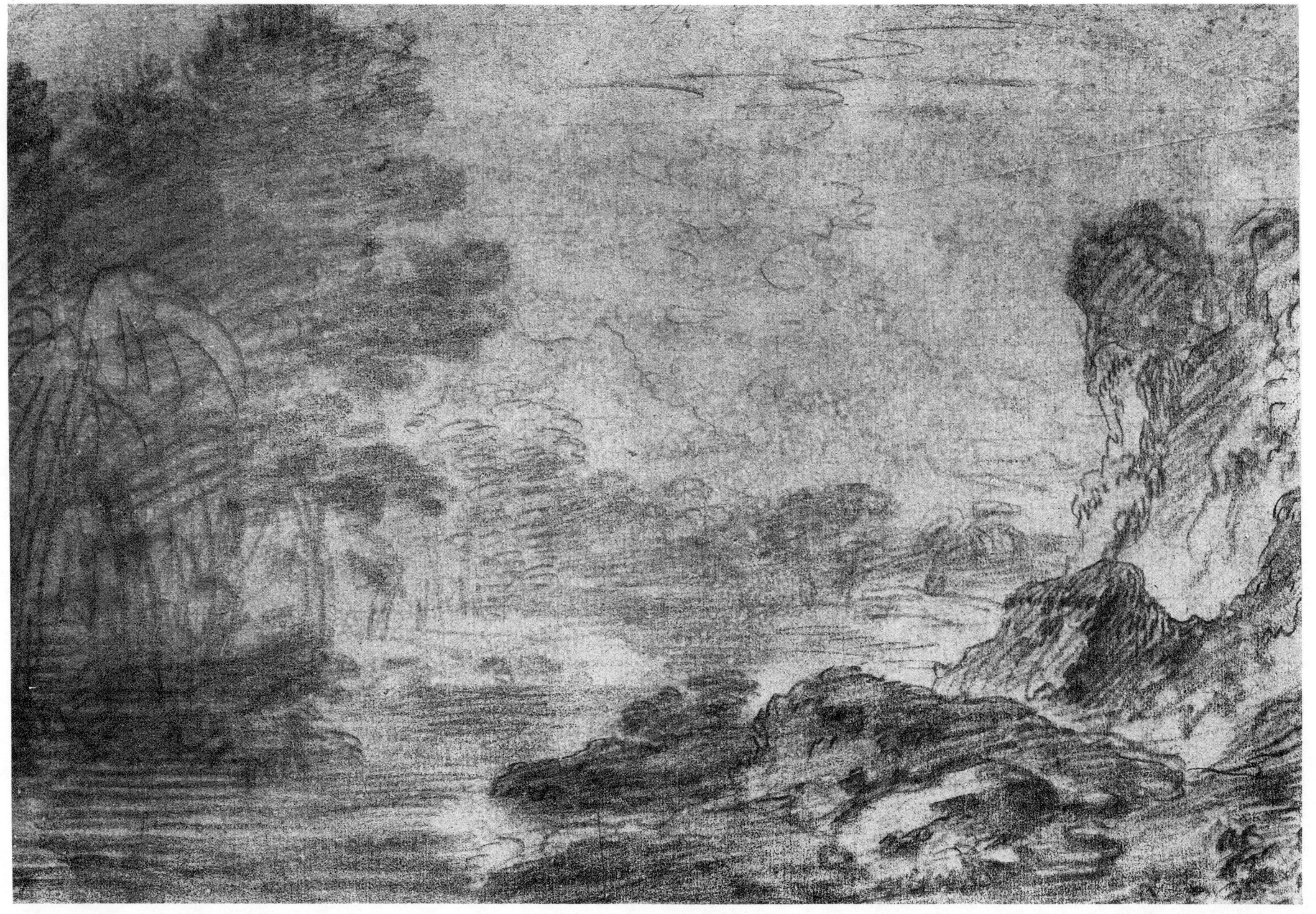

Antoine Watteau (1684–1721). Romantic landscape. Red chalk.

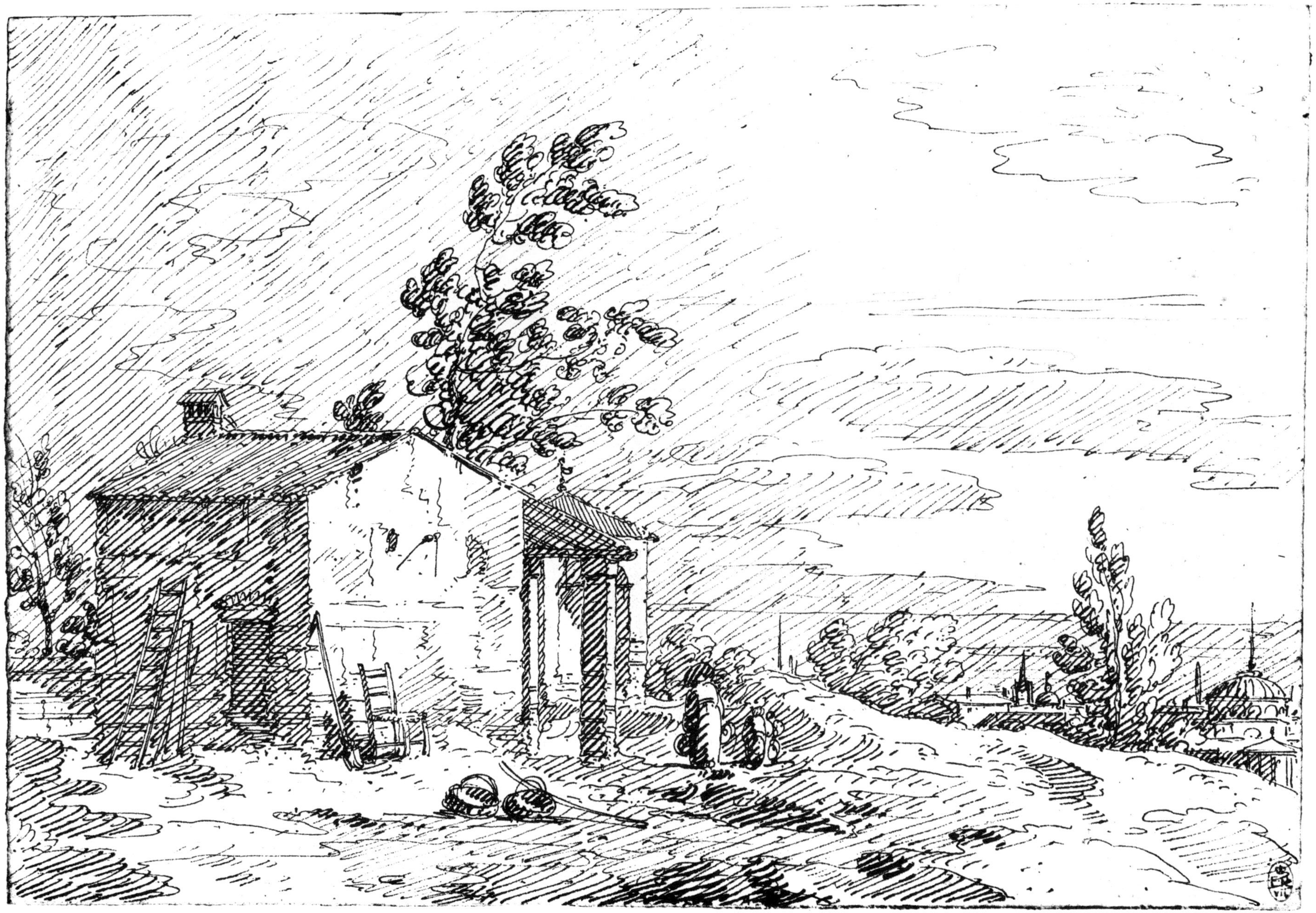

Canaletto (Giovanni Antonio Canal; 1697–1768). Capriccio with a rustic cottage. Pencil, pen and dark brown ink; 189 × 271 mm.

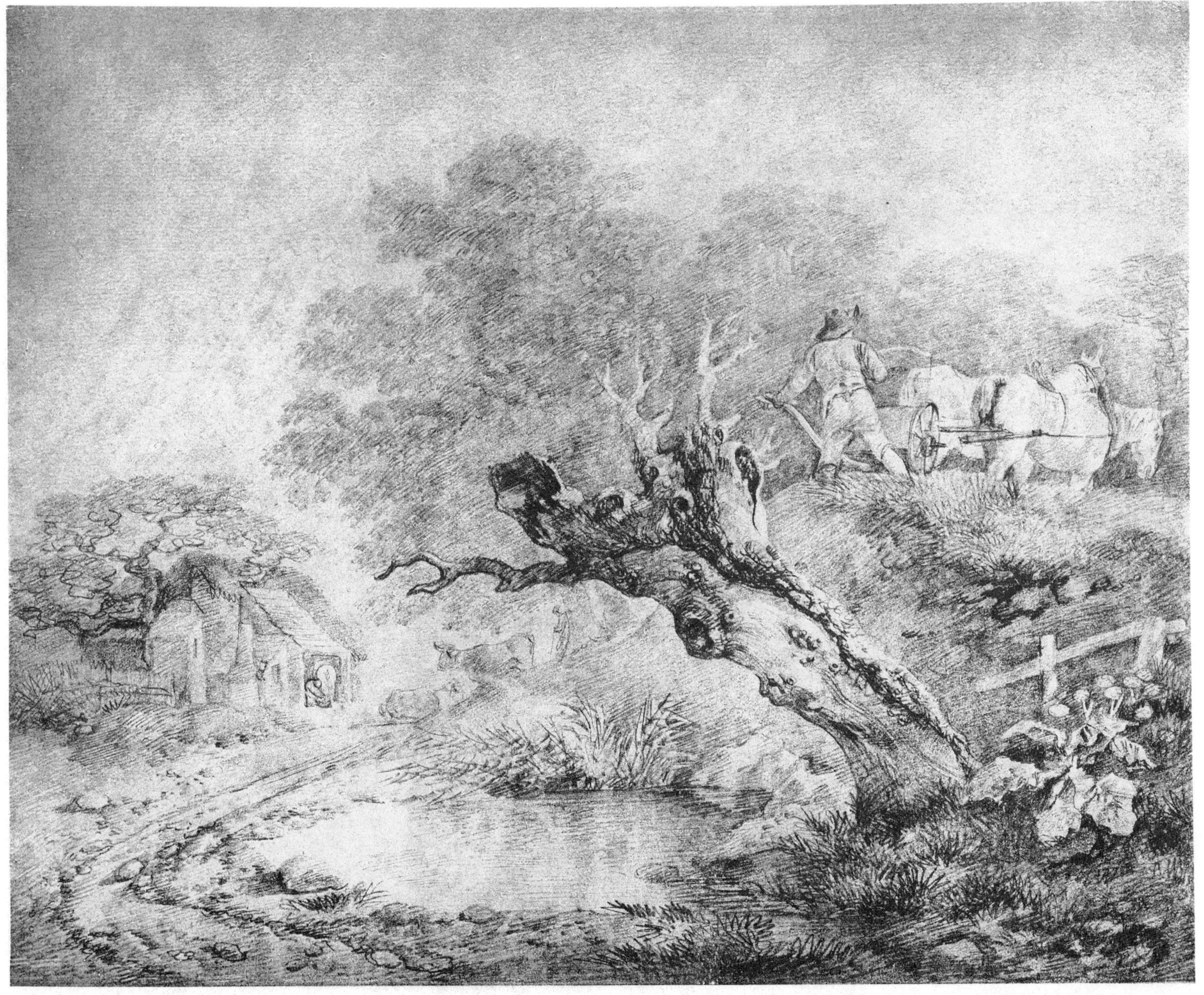

Thomas Gainsborough (1727–1788). Landscape with decayed willow tree. Pencil.

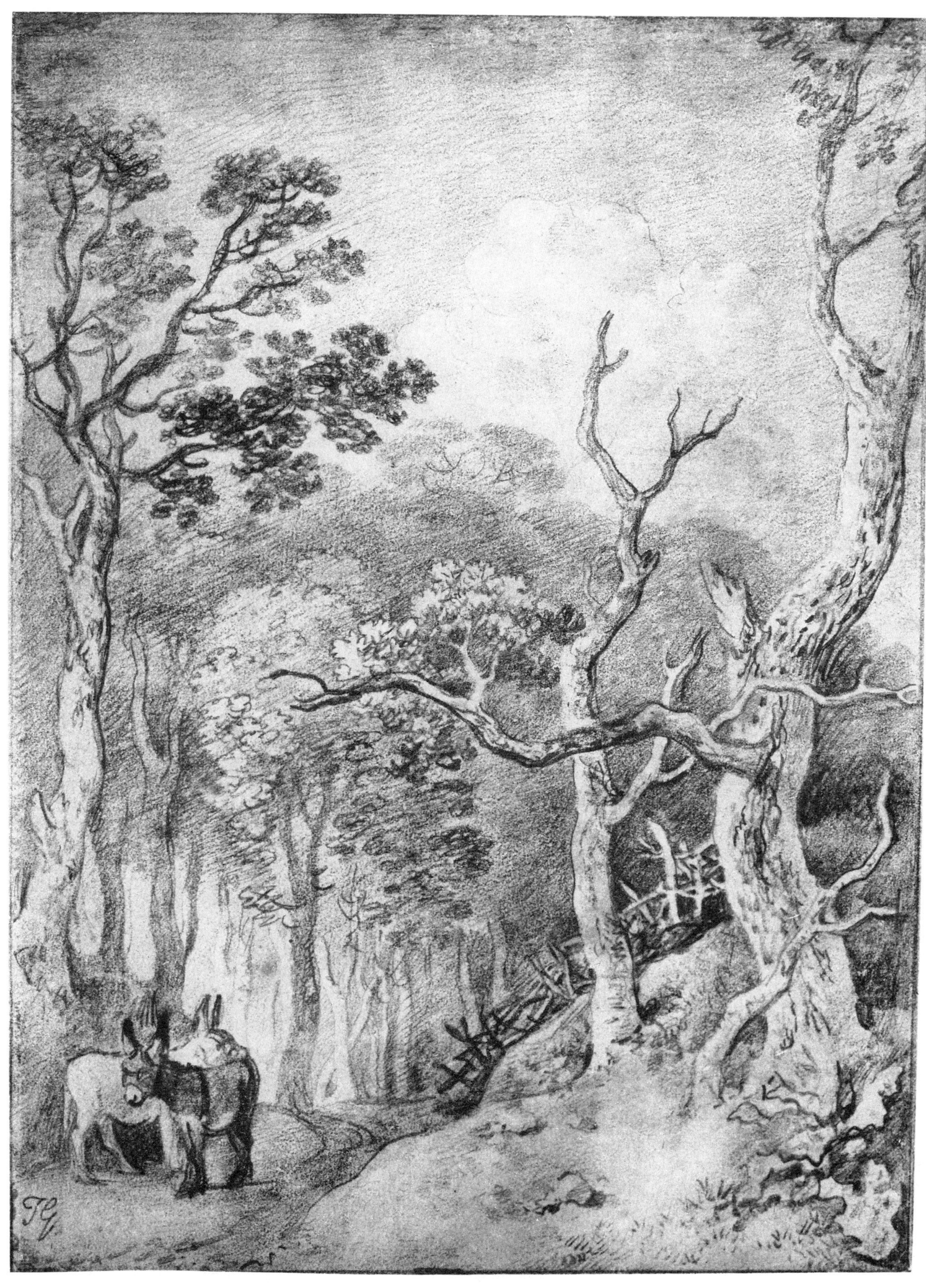

Thomas Gainsborough. Wooded landscape with two donkeys. Pencil.

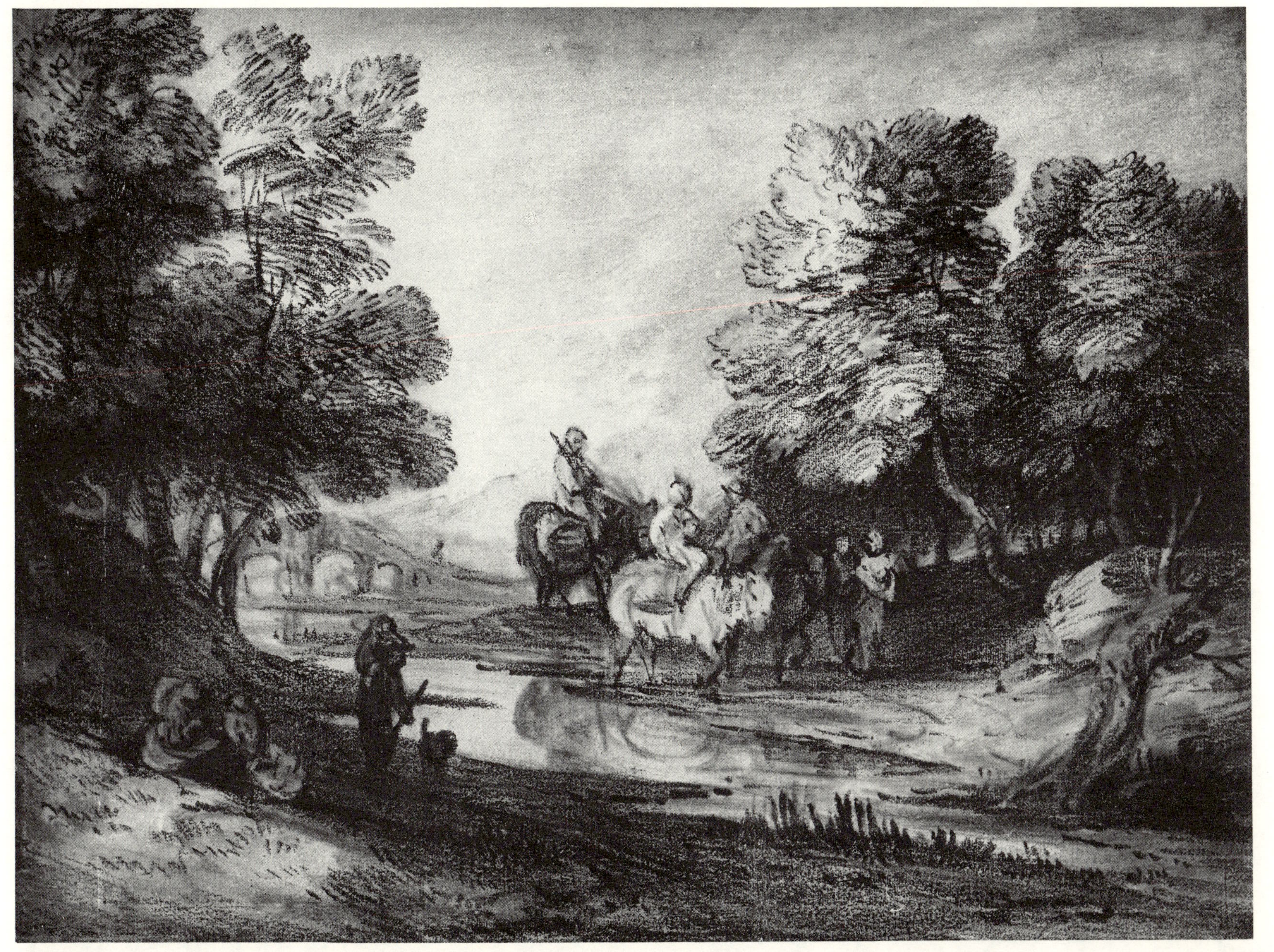

Thomas Gainsborough. River landscape with wooded banks. Black and white chalk.

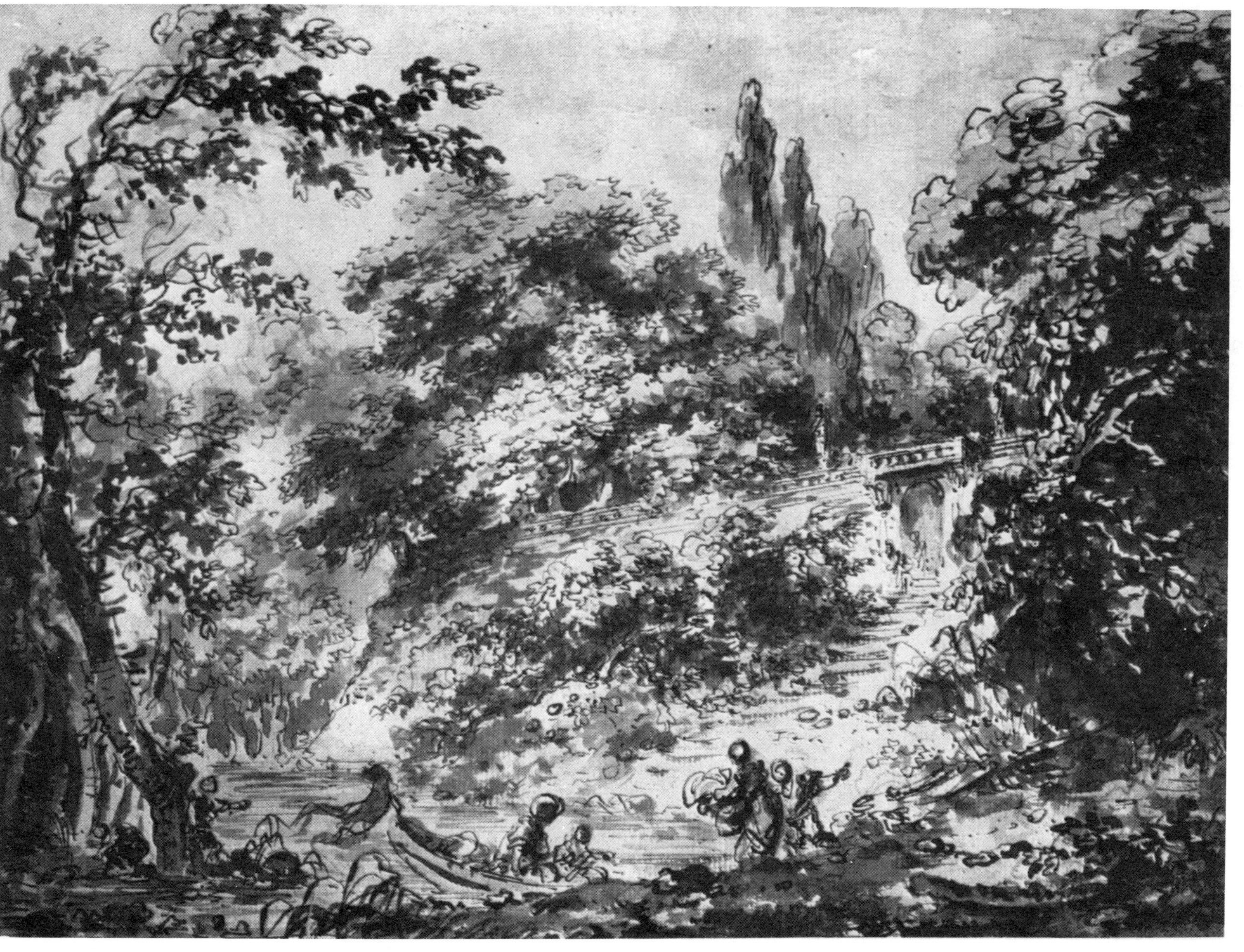

Jean-Honoré Fragonard (1732–1806). Scene in a park. Pen and brush and brown ink, watercolor wash; 193 × 250 mm.

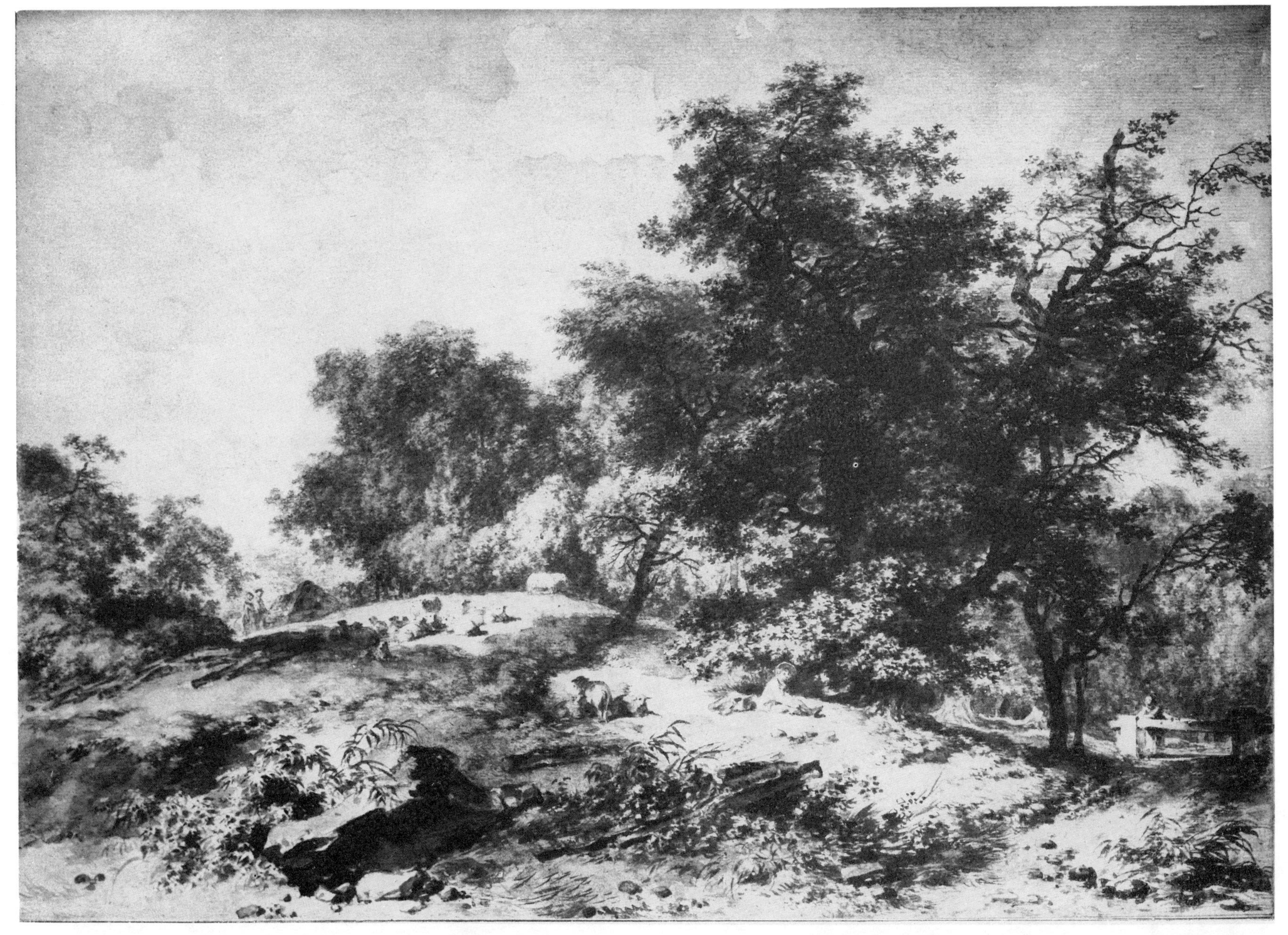

Jean-Honoré Fragonard. Landscape with figures. Pen and bister, washed.

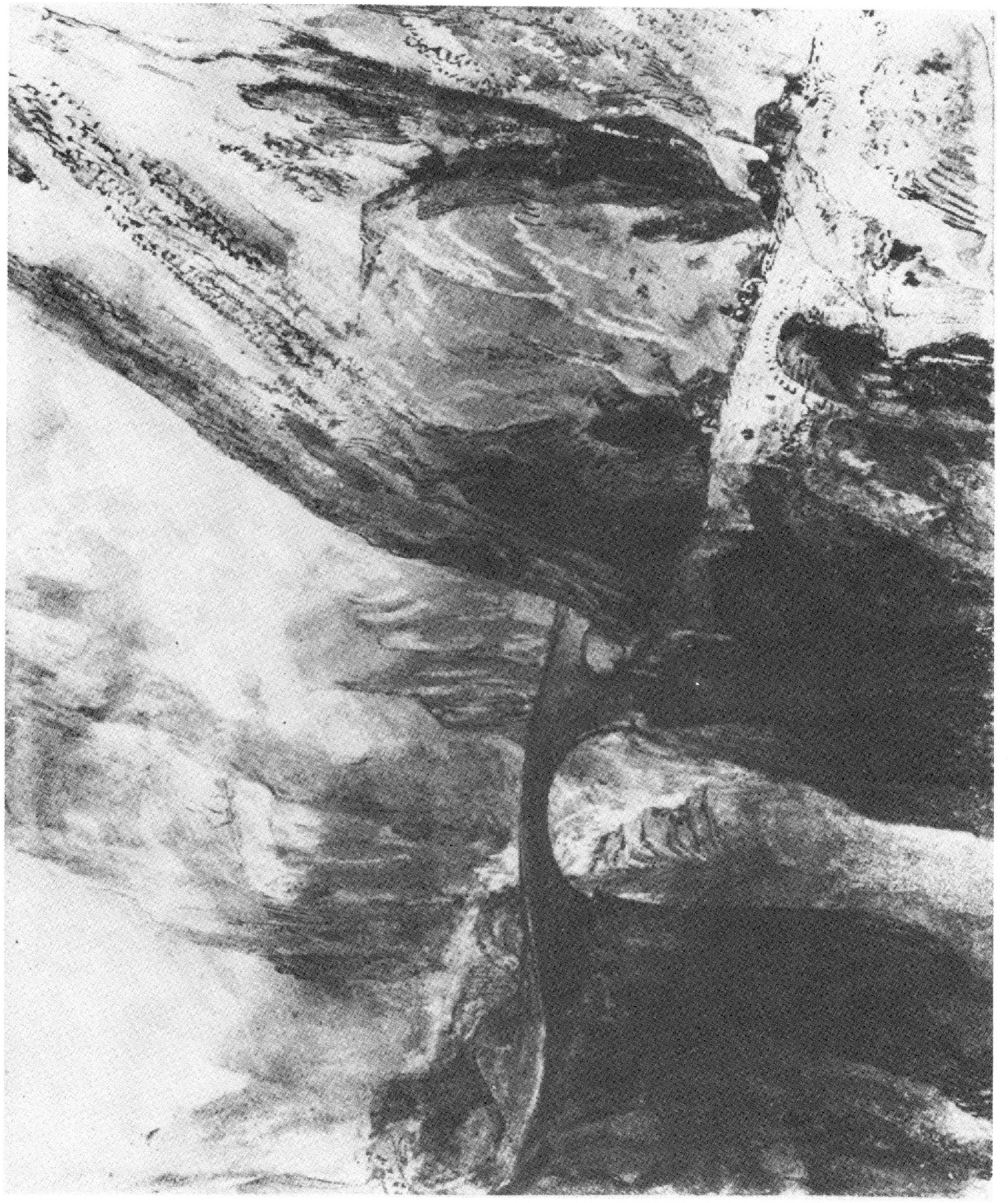

J. M. W. Turner (1775–1851). Saint Gotthard Pass with the Devil's Bridge. Pen and brush and sepia; 215 × 254 mm.

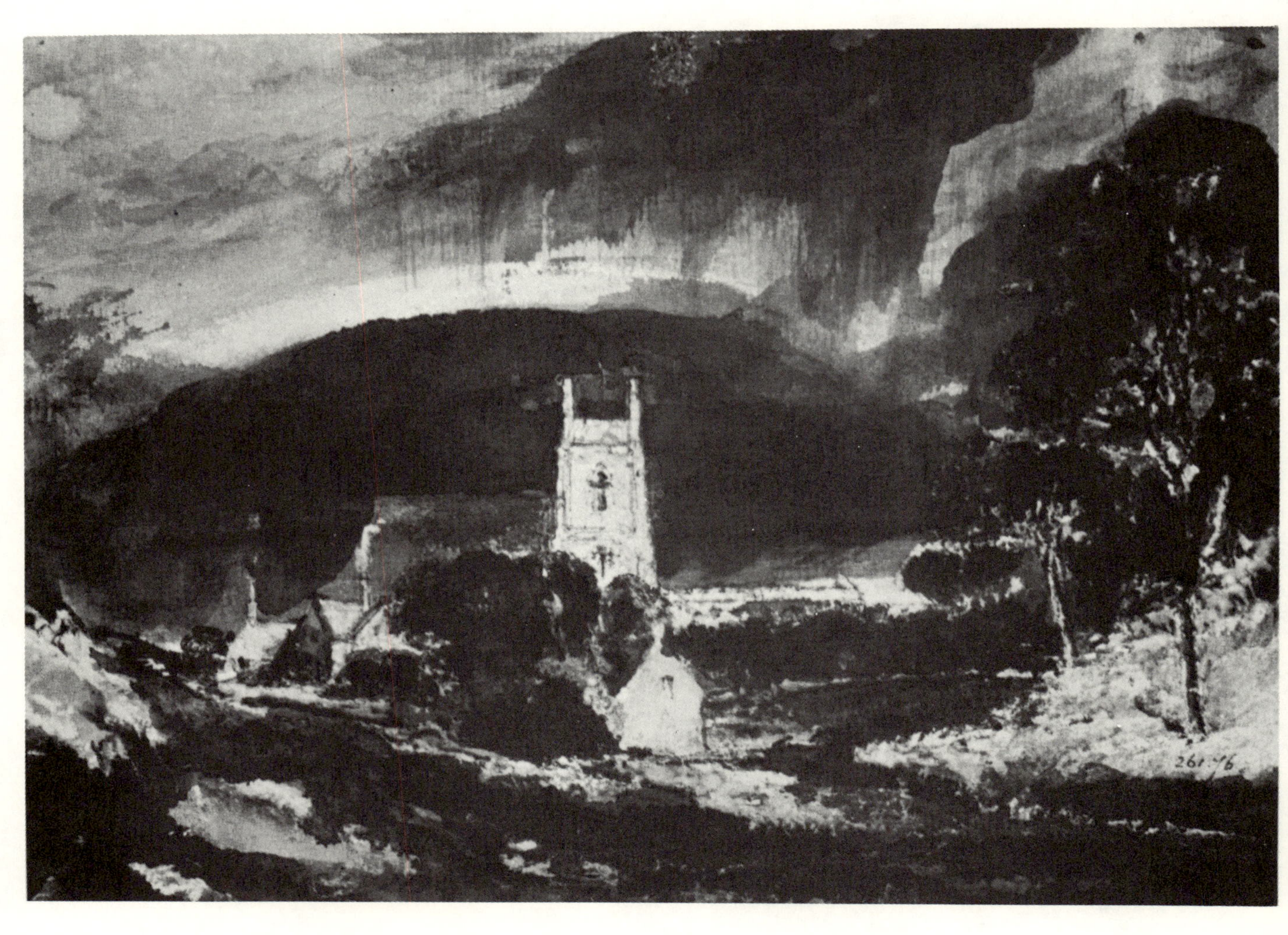

John Constable (1776–1837). Stoke-by-Nayland. Brush and sepia; 127 × 185 mm.

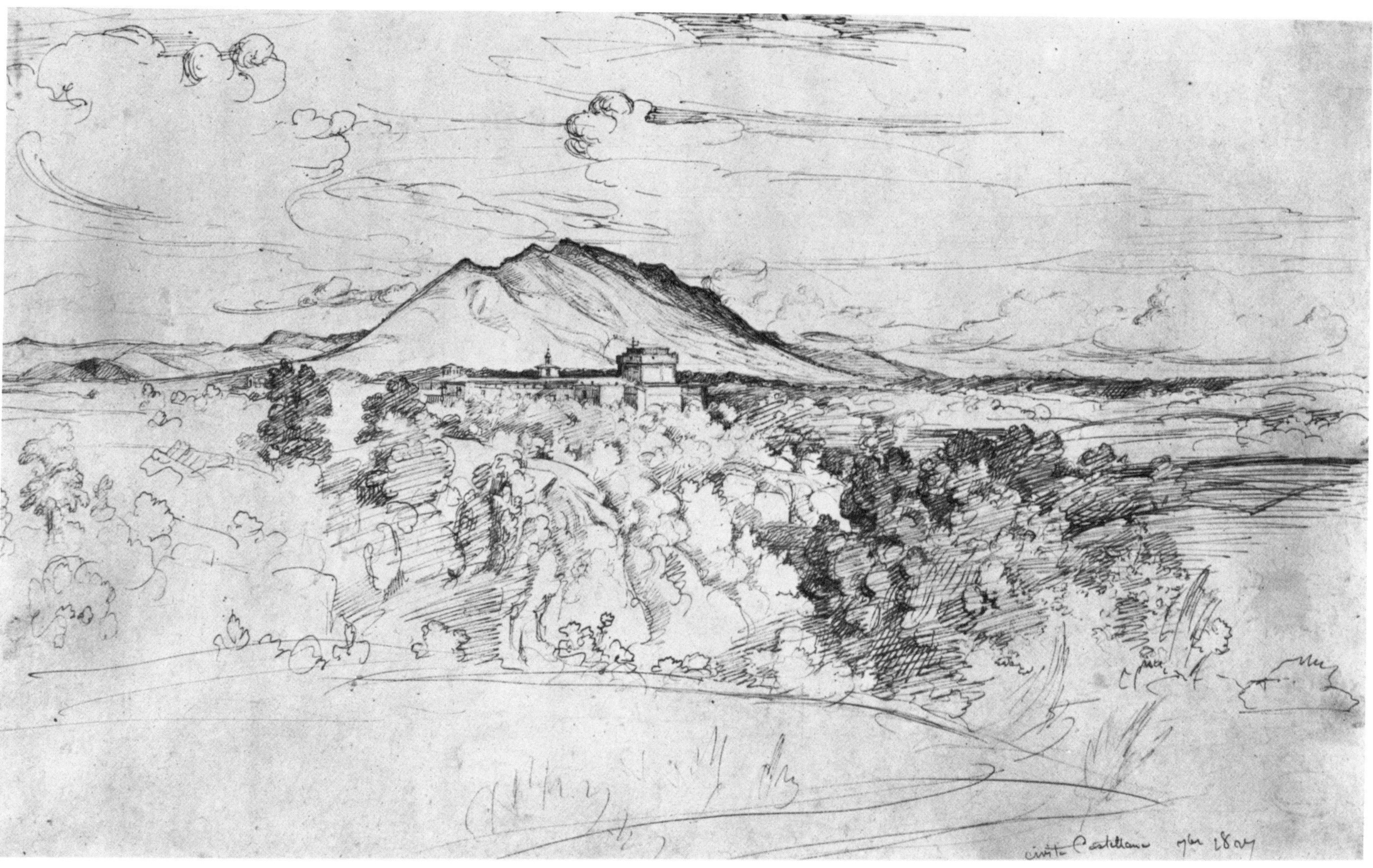

Jean-Baptiste-Camille Corot (1796–1875). Mt. Soracte from Cività Castellana. Pen and ink over pencil; 279 × 416 mm.